Back for a Second Helping . . .

INDIANA'S FAVORITE

HOMETOWN RESTAURANTS

Where the Local Folks Like to Eat

Guild Press of Indiana, Inc.

GUILD PRESS OF INDIANA, INC.
435 Gradle Drive
Carmel, Indiana 46032

ISBN 1-57860-042-1
Library of Congress
Catalog Card Number
99-67153

*All illustrations and cover art and design by David Bartholomew,
Two-Headed Graphics, Fishers, Indiana*

Text designed by Sheila G. Samson

Printed and bound in the United States of America

Contents

Reader support spawns this new, improved edition of Indiana's Favorite Hometown Restaurants

This book was never meant to be. When the first edition was published in 1995, fifteen hundred copies were printed. We prayed that we could sell that number—enough to recover our costs. Production of a new edition was the furthest thing from our minds.

But thanks to news media attention and word-of-mouth advertisement from readers, we were besieged with requests for more, and sales of the first book escalated to five thousand. When supplies were exhausted in 1998, we continued to receive enthusiastic encouragement to either print more or publish a new edition. It was this public support as expressed in many complimentary letters and telephone requests that was the deciding factor in fostering this, the second edition of *Indiana's Favorite Hometown Restaurants*.

This new publication also would not have been possible without the persistent encouragement of a true believer, Nancy Baxter, president of Guild Press of Indiana, and the pleadings of our diligent office manager, Sue Whitaker, as well as the guidance and wit of our communications director Mike Roeder and his writer-wife, Lee Ann Weitzel Roeder.

The new edition is bigger and, we hope, better. The process of selecting the restaurants, however, remains essentially the same. Local elected officials and the much-traveled staff of the Association of Cities and Towns nominated all the restaurants listed. Not all recommendations were selected, however. The selection criteria favored locally owned and operated restaurants that have at least one outstanding feature. No "chain" restaurants were accepted. To assure objectivity in the preparation of the book, there is no advertising, nor were any endorsements considered.

We hope you agree that this new edition is an improvement. We have more than seventy additional restaurant listings and much more information, fascinating historic facts and out-of-the-way visitor attractions. The hundreds of restaurants in this edition are presented in six segments representing Indiana's tourism regions: Central, South Central, Southern, Western, Northern, and Eastern. Each segment opens with an overview on the visitor attractions in and near the communities where restaurants are listed. Many of the visitor attractions suggested may not be found in the major tour books, but were selected because of unique characteristics. For instance, we found that county and regional historical museums such as the Daviess County Museum, located in an old school house near Washington, and the Fulton County Round Barn Museum near Rochester contain displays as fascinating in their own local way as those in big-city facilities. And admission is often free although donations are always "gratefully accepted."

One new feature throughout this edition is a reflection of the sudden emergence of the Internet as an aid to consumers in the dining and tourism industry. You might say about the Internet, "Everywhere you go, there it is." There was not a single Internet web site listed in our first edition, but nowadays the Net has become an almost indispensable tool for the frequent traveler/diner. Five of the Top Ten dining establishments in this book feature web sites which allow the visitor to browse the menu, study the history of the facility or, in the case of Jasper's The Schnitzelbank, listen to "The Chicken Song" while planning your visit to the popular eatery.

Many of the visitor attractions and most convention bureaus, too, have informative web sites with links to local attractions, lodging and dining establishments. One web site, Shapiro's Restaurant and Deli in Indianapolis, allows Internet travelers to order anything from a corned beef sandwich to a sack of double chocolate chunk cookies in advance via FAX. We have included as many web site addresses as we could find in this current edition of *Indiana's Favorite Hometown Restaurants*. Whether it's an evening out at your favorite dining establishment or a journey of several days, the Internet can be a valuable tool especially when used as a companion to this book.

Michael J. Quinn, executive director
Indiana Association of Cities & Towns

Use this book to discover restful,
inexpensive ways to tour Indiana

We hope you will use this book. Keep one in the family sedan and let it be your guide to planning a day trip to see that undiscovered part of Indiana you've been longing to visit.

Whether you're walking the labyrinth and viewing the restored remnants of two utopian communities at historic New Harmony, dancing and dining through the swirling excitement of downtown Indianapolis, or savoring the culinary excellence and quality craftsmanship of Indiana's Amish communities, there's lots to see and do in Indiana.

The coming of the new millennium has fostered activities that have sparked heightened interest in Hoosier heritage. And those who pursue Hoosier history and cultural attractions are finding the quest rewarding in several ways. First, it's always fun to learn interesting facts about the place where we live. Second, Indiana visitor attractions can be reached via good roads and enjoyed without the glut of crowds and high costs often found at major entertainment facilities.

The relatively low cost of living in the Hoosier state keeps prices at many restaurants, visitor attractions and lodging facilities at reasonable levels. For instance, the most popular meal at the number one hometown restaurant in Indiana is less than ten dollars. And the summertime weekday rate at one of Indiana's most charming and distinctive lodging establishments, the Artists Colony Inn at Nashville, is less than a hundred dollars. A visit to one of Indiana's most scenic historic sites, the T. C. Steele home, "The House of the Singing Winds," and his adjacent art-filled studio at Belmont, is free.

Thus, with prudent planning, you shouldn't have to mortgage the mini-barn to pay for an outing in Hoosierland.

Happy Hoosier Trails!

How to use this guide

The listings of restaurants in this book are arranged by region and municipality. Included in each listing are the restaurant's address, phone, whether credit cards are accepted, and days of the week and hours open. We've provided a summary highlighting favorite meals, house specialties, and sometimes a bit of history about the restaurant.

The following abbreviations are used throughout this guide:

Days of the week
Su, M, T, W, Th, F, S

Credit card abbreviations
MC = MasterCard
V = Visa
AmEx = American Express
Di = Discover
DC = Diners Club

The Song of the Guide Book

O sing a song of the Guide Book,
    The book of motoring miles;
Look at the map at Stony Gap,
    Turn east at the Lumber Piles.
You Jog Left here, you Jog Right there,
    Cross R. R. at Mandelay;
At set of sun — Oh, boy, you've done
    Three hundred and one today!

You hit the hay at Slumbertown,
    You're up at the break of dawn;
You need more sleep, but that can keep —
    You grab an egg and are gone.
Follow the poles to Jimsonville,
    Turn north at thirty-one-three;
Go down the hill to Mauzy's Mill,
    Jog Left at the Willow Tree.

You find a Main Street everywhere,
    There are Broadways by the score;
Signs "Welcome" you, signs say adieu —
    Then the Open Road once more.
You halt at Daubenspeck's Garage
    For gasoline, oil and air,
Then grab a bite — Jog Left, Jog Right, —
    And the Guide Book says you're There!

So sing a song of the Guide Book,
    The book of motoring miles;
The book that made a joy-parade
    And banished your sighs with smiles.
When Winter's pent-up days are here
    You'll get the old Guide Book down,
Jog Left, Jog Right in Fancy's flight
    To your own dear Old Home Town!

— William Herschell
The Indianapolis News, August 19, 1922

INDIANA'S FAVORITE
HOMETOWN RESTAURANTS

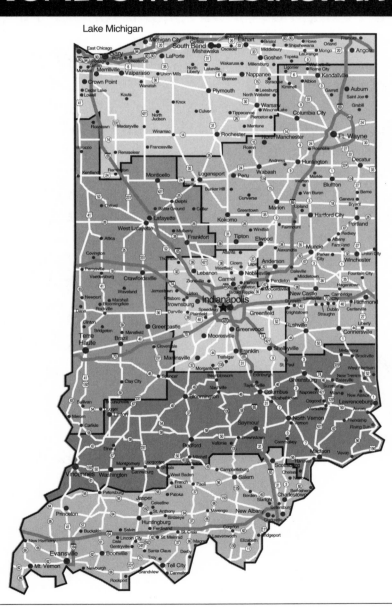

Lake Michigan

Fried Chicken is King Among Top Ten Picks

The chicken wins! Among Indiana's favorite hometown restaurants, chicken is king!

Of the featured menu items of the top two restaurants, The Log Inn in Warrenton and Das Dutchman Essenhaus in Middlebury, most proponents commented on the extraordinary quality of the fried chicken.

The fried chicken at three other Top Ten dining establishments also drew the crows of praise from hometown customers: the Overlook Restaurant at Leavenworth, the Schnitzelbank at Jasper, and Welliver's at Hagerstown.

Beef came in second with the steaks at St. Elmo Steak House in Indianapolis, and at The Beef House near Covington — ranked as the best in Indiana.

While several fine restaurants throughout the state feature catfish, the hometown folks had a clear choice in The Waverly Inn, southwest of Indianapolis.

The top turkey restaurant also was a unanimous pick — The Strongbow Turkey Inn at Valparaiso.

As for the top pork tenderloin sandwich, the fan mail is heaviest about Mr. Dave's at North Manchester.

Traditional tastes and family values are reflected in Top Ten Restaurant picks

HOOSIERS ARE SAID TO BE FOLKS with old-fashioned family values and no-nonsense tastes. Those basic truths were reflected in the selections for the second edition of Indiana's Favorite Hometown Restaurants' Top Ten list, with the state's oldest eatery leading an epicurean parade of mostly traditional fried-chicken and steak-and-mashed-potato-style dining establishments which dominated the best of Hoosierland's restaurants. And family-owned-and-operated dining facilities were a distinct favorite among the local folks who cast the ballots.

1
The Log Inn, Warrenton

The oldest is now the best. The historic Log Inn near Haubstadt in scenic southwest Indiana moves up from its second place position in the 1995 edition of *Favorite Hometown Restaurants* to the top of the menu as Indiana's most popular hometown restaurant.

Excellent food, served efficiently and inexpensively in a 165-year-old authentic pioneer atmosphere rich in Indiana history, are the basic ingredients in the Log Inn's recipe for its success and popularity. The restaurant provides its most priceless menu selection—the family style fried chicken dinner—at less than $10.00.

Owned and operated since 1978 by Gene and Rita Elpers, the unpretentious dining establishment is located one mile east of U.S. 41 on Old State Road near Warrenton about 12 miles north of Evansville.

Constructed as a stagecoach stop in 1825, the 500-seat facility continues to transport visitors on a trip back in time with plank floors and rough-hewn log walls and wood-beamed ceilings. The Log Inn is believed to be the oldest restaurant in continuous operation in Indiana. It has been documented that Abraham Lincoln visited there in 1844 on his way home to Illinois from Evansville, where he'd been campaigning for Henry Clay. On that same trip he had also visited his mother's grave in Spencer County. Ask to be seated in the Lincoln Room where the Great Emancipator dined.

During the Civil War, a cellar in the original log cabin was a stop on the Underground Railroad.

The trip turns into an adventure in Hoosier dining when the menu is presented. While ala carte entrees are available, family style dining is the attraction for gatherings of three or more. In addition to what many believe to be Indiana's tastiest fried chicken, family style options include ham or roast beef. Meals are served with mountains of mashed potatoes, gravy, two vegetables (we liked the hot German potato salad and the red cabbage), slaw and rolls. For $1.00 extra the Elpers will throw in an order of their delicious German fries. Prices are $9.75 for adults and $4.75 for children. (Alcoholic beverages are available.)

Among the nominators is Clerk-Treasurer Bonnie Wagner, from nearby Haubstadt, who heads a growing number of Hoosier dining fans who have declared that The Log Inn's fried chicken is, "the best."

Bring cash or a checkbook, as The Log Inn does not accept credit cards. Reservations are accepted.

RR 2, Haubstadt 47639
(812) 867-3216
Open: 4–9 p.m. T–Th, 4–10 p.m. F–S, closed Su–M

2 Das Dutchman Essenhaus, Middlebury

Das Dutchman Essenhaus zooms from tenth place in our 1995 restaurant guide to second best. But, you may ask, what is an "essenhaus?" Is it one of Indiana's largest family restaurants? An outstanding bakery? A unique shopping experience? Or an Amish Country Inn? You guessed it—Das Dutchman Essenhaus is, indeed, all of the above. It is what we call the "Essenhaus Experience."

Opened by Bob and Sue Miller in 1970, the family continues to provide outstanding food and service to as many as eleven hundred dining guests at one time. It is, indeed, Indiana's largest family restaurant. On a busy day, the northern Indiana facility serves about eight thousand guests. Most famous for their all-you-care-to eat family style meals of chicken, roast beef, baked steak and ham, diners also receive mashed potatoes and gravy, dressing, noodles, hot vegetables, tossed salads with one of their eight homemade salad dressings (we like the sweet and sour dressing), bread, and apple butter. The highly popular chicken dinners are $11.65 per person. And, don't be foolish enough to skip dessert.

Few would challenge that the Essenhaus homemade pies are the best anywhere. At less than $3.00 a slice, it's a bargain. Try the Red Raspberry Cream pie and stop at the bakery on the way out to take one home. While we are primarily concerned with the cuisine, visitors will find much at the Essenhaus village of shops and facilities to keep them there long before and after the memorable meals. Bring the kids because the new Sunshine Farms offers youngsters a chance to interact with farm animals, ride a pony and pet miniature horses. Also, overnight accommodations are available at the 33-room Essenhaus Country Inn, constructed to resemble a white Amish farmhouse. The Inn is tastefully furnished with the handmade crafts of Amish artisans.

For a pleasant after-meal diversion, we suggest a browsing tour at the nearby Village Shops located in four adjacent farm buildings, where unusual items include handmade Amish dolls. And for a sneak preview of your visit, drop in on their Internet web site to learn more about the total "Essenhaus Experience," including full menus, shopping, overnight accommodations, mail-order purchases and much more colorfully presented information: **www.essenhaus.com**. We suggest you call ahead for reservations. Das Dutchman Essenhaus is a non-smoking dining establishment and does not serve alcoholic beverages. The facility is located about 15 minutes east of Elkhart and just west of Middlebury on U.S. 20.

240 US 20, Middlebury 46540
(219) 825-9472 or toll-free at (800) 455-9471
Open: 6 a.m.–8 p.m. M–Th, 6 a.m.–9 p.m. F–S, closed Su
MC V Di

3
The Beef House, Covington

The Beef House, selected as the best restaurant in the state last time around, is another outstanding family-owned-and-operated dining establishment which continues as a top favorite of local folks. Named "Best Steak House in Indiana" by *Midwest Living* magazine, the spacious restaurant remains Number One in the hearts and appetites of many ardent Beef House customers such as Middletown Councilmember Dallas

Hunter who proclaimed in his nomination "My very favorite place to eat even though it is 100 miles away." Hunter's favorite taste treat is the house charcoal-broiled sirloin steak with baked potato and a full plate from the lavish salad bar. Hunter and others like Brazil Mayor Ken Crabb are enthusiastic in their praise of the friendly atmosphere and delectable array of dining options available at this user-friendly facility.

Owned and operated by three generations of the Wright family for nearly four decades, proprietors Bob and Bonnie Wright have been joined by their children and grandchildren in creating a pleasant dining experience. Nominators also praise the friendly and efficient table service and some of the best steaks you'll find anywhere. How good are the steaks? Well, the restaurant has been named the "Best of Beef" restaurant in Indiana by the Indiana Beef Council. 'Nuff said? Trademark of The Beef House is the yeast rolls, best experienced with the fresh jam provided at each table. Bob Wright devised the recipe for the rolls while a restaurant management student at Purdue University. Now, thousands of Purdue fans traveling to and from events at nearby West Lafayette are reaping the rewards of Bob's academic and culinary achievements. Our favorite continues to be the unequaled filet mignon although many favor the rib eye steak or, for heartier appetites, the 20-ounce T-bone. The recommendation for an appetizer is the frog legs prepared with garlic butter. The soups are made fresh daily with the broccoli and chicken rice remaining a top choice with veteran Beef House enthusiasts.

Reservations are recommended, although the 500-seat capacity makes waiting a rarity. (Reservations are not accepted on Saturday.) Nonsmoking seating is available, as are alcoholic beverages, including an extensive wine list. All major credit cards are accepted.

Located on the NW corner of Indiana SR 63 and I-74 (exit #4) about four
miles west of Covington
(765) 793-3947
Open: 8 a.m.–10 p.m. M–F, 2:30–10:30p.m.S, 11 a.m.–9 p.m. Su

4
St. Elmo Steak House, Indianapolis

Despite the incursion in Indianapolis of numerous new "chain" restaurants featuring steak and other red meat delicacies, the venerable St. Elmo Steak House, in the booming heart of the downtown of the Capital City, was selected as the fourth favorite choice among local officials, thus returning it to our Top Ten. The historic dining establishment remains a strong favorite with local officials visiting Indianapolis who continue to favor the traditional steak house atmosphere.

Now approaching 100 years of continuous operation, most regulars rave about the Jumbo Shrimp Cocktails with homemade horseradish sauce and, of course, the mouth-watering steaks. It's expensive and can be noisy when there's a full house of diners, but most local government officials are accustomed to such surroundings and usually include a night at St. Elmo's when in Indianapolis. St. Elmo's is open seven days a week—but don't even think of arriving without a reservation. All major creidt cards accepted.

> **127 S. Illinois St., Indianapolis 46225**
> **(317) 635-0636**
> **Open: 4–10:30 p.m.M–S, 5–9:30 p.m. Su**

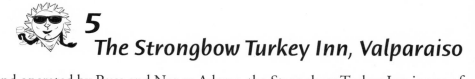

5
The Strongbow Turkey Inn, Valparaiso

Owned and operated by Russ and Nancy Adams, the Strongbow Turkey Inn is one of the few facilities of its kind to feature turkey entrees.

Now starting the fourth generation of the Adams family to operate this historic dining establishment, The Strongbow has a growing clientele as indicated by its rise since the first edition of *Indiana's Favorite Hometown Restaurants* from an honorable mention to fifth place. Named for the Potawatomi Indian chief who once lived on the land with his many wives, The Strongbow Turkey Inn first opened in 1940 and now produces the best in native Hoosier dining.

A favorite of Valparaiso Mayor David Butterfield is the Strongbow Turkey Dinner. Other favorites are the turkey pie and smoked turkey wings. Our choice for a unique taste treat is the Strongbow Schnitzel, a classic Wienerschnitzel using breast of turkey (instead of veal) served in a lemon-butter sauce.

The menu also features daily specials. The dessert menu boasts some of the most enticing treats you'll find anywhere, including Triple Orange Cake and French Silk Pie. The Inn now boasts its own full-service bakery which produces scrumptious pies, cakes and the restaurant's highly popular yeast rolls, served with all dinners. Few visitors can depart without a "take home" supply of the succulent baked goods. Alcoholic beverages are available.

For delicious details, including a complete history of the inn, visit the restaurant's web site: **www.strongbowinn.com**. Dress is casual to dressy. Reservations are accepted, as are all major credit cards.

> **2405 US 30 E, Valparaiso 46383 (at the intersection of SR 49)**
> **(219) 462-5121 or toll free (800) 462-5121.**
> **Open: 11 a.m.–9 p.m. M–F, 11 a.m.–9:30 S, 11 a.m.–8:30 p.m. Su**

6
The Overlook Restaurant and Lounge, Leavenworth

With perhaps the most beautiful view and tastiest fried chicken in these parts, The Overlook Restaurant and Lounge is located on a bluff high above the curving oxbow bend of the Ohio River.

Like others in the Top Ten, The Overlook has a proud history of serving guests for more than 50 years. Along with the fried chicken, it's the homemade biscuits and pies—made fresh daily—that owners Doug and Josie Breeden claim keep their customers coming back. Service, too, is stressed in their motto: "The only thing we overlook is the view."

Beams and planks from an old barn were used to decorate the interior as part of a recent expansion, appropriately called "the Barn Room." The improvements also included a huge deck which provides a relaxing perch for absorbing the 20-mile view of the river's bend.

Another well-deserved newcomer to the coveted *Favorite Hometown Restaurants'* Top Ten, The Overlook also is keeping up with the times by offering customers a preview of its delightful dining experiences via the Internet. Their web site, **www.theoverlook.com**, also provides Net surfers with suggestions on local visitor attractions such as Provisions Gift Shop, their next-door neighbor. All major credit cards accepted.

> **State Road 62, Leavenworth 47137**
> **(812) 739-4264**
> **Open: 8 a.m.–9 p.m. daily (closed Christmas Eve and Day)**

7
The Schnitzelbank, Jasper

A newcomer to the *Favorite Hometown Restaurants* honor roll, The Schnitzelbank Restaurant—"A Little Bit of Germany" in southern Indiana—is widely known for its authentic German food and friendly atmosphere.

However, The Schnitzelbank is no stranger to residents of the region and elsewhere. Owned and operated by three generations of the Hanselman family, the spacious facility is located on the site of a beer hall built in 1903 and continues the tradition of providing the very best in German cuisine and beverages in an atmosphere decorated with colorful family shields, banners, and wooden beams. Look and listen for the dining establishment's landmark—a musical Glockenspiel tower, high above the restaurant building, that plays the original Schnitzelbank song on the hour.

And the food itself is a symphony of culinary compositions. Local folks favor the kraut balls as an appetizer. In addition to nightly specials, eleven German dishes are standard offerings on the menu with a favorite of many being the beef Rolladen. Other local favorites include the hickory-smoked pork chops and the sauerbraten. Also among the best is . . . the Wurst—a steaming hot selection of sausages served on a bed of sauerkraut with German fries. However, Jasper Mayor Bill Schmitt dares to be different in his own hometown. His Honor's favorite? Fried chicken.

A necessary ingredient in a truly authentic German-American dinner at the Schnitzelbank is a chilled glass of *Brau*. Our suggestion? Try any one of the more than 50 imported beers or the Schnitzel Weiss, a German wheat beer brewed especially for the restaurant. Top off your Rhineland dining experience with the hot apple strudel or the German chocolate pie. Most major credit cards honored.

The Schnitzelbank also offers daily early bird specials from 4 to 6 p.m. And before departing, browse in the popular gift shop where you'll find an enticing selection of beer steins, local crafts, and selections from local wineries.

393 Third Ave., Jasper 47546
(812) 482-2640 / FAX (812) 482-7687
Web Site: www.schnitzelbank.com
Open: 6 a.m.–9 p.m. M–S, closed Su

8
The Waverly Inn, Waverly

The Waverly Inn, southwest of Indianapolis, proudly boasts that it offers diners "the best catfish in Indiana."

While that title may be challenged by other proud purveyors of the whiskered wonders, we have several well-satisfied diners who swear this fish story is true. And owner Allen Culpepper is proud of the fact that the establishment is approaching its thirtieth consecutive year of successful operation.

Besides catfish, The Waverly Inn also features an all-you-care-to-eat salad bar. And save room for "The Waverly Delight"— a hot chocolate fudge sundae nestled atop a brownie, the restaurant's most popular dessert. All major credit cards are honored.

located about 15 minutes south of I-465 on SR 37
(about 17 miles south of Indianapolis and 10 miles north of Martinsville)
(317) 422-9368.
Open 11 a.m.–9 p.m. M–Th, 11 a.m.–10 p.m. F–S, noon–9 p.m. Su

9
Shapiro's Delicatessen Cafeteria, Indianapolis

Another historic landmark just south of downtown Indianapolis which drew votes from across the state is Shapiro's Delicatessen Cafeteria, where office workers mingle with local residents, corporate executives and tourists to savor the kosher-style delicacies of this ninety-four-year-old institution.

Four generations of the Shapiro family have combined to produce what many culinary observers have hailed as the nation's best corned beef sandwich. Using Shapiro's extensive web site, **www.shapiros.com**, busy diners can check the menu selection and then send their to-go orders ahead via FAX. The web site also offers visitors a glimpse at the intriguing history of the now-thriving business begun by Russian immigrants in 1905. Other moderately priced taste treats include the stuffed cabbage and chopped steak with the obligatory *latke* — a crispy potato pancake.

Bagels abound, from blueberry to spinach-flavored, as do a dazzling array of desserts. Among the local favorites are butterscotch praline and sweet potato pies.

You'll be a hit at home if you grab a sack of homemade cookies to go from the carry-out counter. The Heath toffee, oatmeal raisin, and chocolate chunk cookies are a special taste treat. A newer version of the original facility with the same appealing menu can be found on the Northwestside of the city. Cash only at both sites.

DOWNTOWN: **808 S. Meridian St.**
(317) 631-4041 / FAX 631-3958
Open: 6:30 a.m. –8:30 p.m. daily

NORTHWESTSIDE: **2370 W. 86th St.**
(317) 872-7255 / FAX 875-8666
Open: 6:30 a.m.–9 p.m. daily

10
Welliver's Smorgasbord, Hagerstown

Welliver's Smorgasbord has been providing the best in smorgasbord dining since 1946, and is another unique dining establishment paying a return visit to the *Favorite Hometown Restaurants'* Top Ten.

Specialties abound, but the Welliver's experience should begin by attacking one of the iced mounds of peel-and-eat shrimp. Save room, however, because the shrimp is just one of 75 enticing items on the salad bar and there are a total of 150 items on the full-service buffet. Most regulars favor the skillet fried country chicken, aided by a cup of the cream of onion soup and abetted by a slice or two of homemade cinnamon bread.

When planning your visit, keep in mind that Welliver's is open only Thursday through Sunday. Average meal cost is $10–$15, and all major credit cards are honored. (Note: A pleasant stroll over to Abbott's Candy Shop, 48 E. Walnut St., after dinner might be good for your health and your sweet tooth. The Abbott family has been producing fine caramels and other delicacies for three generations.)

40 E. Main St., Hagerstown 47346
(765) 489-4131
Open: Thurs., 4:30–8 p.m. Th, 4:30–8:30 p.m. F,
4–9 p.m. S, 11 a.m.–8 p.m. Su, closed M–W

Honorable Mention

(Information about these restaurants appears in the regional description, on the pages as noted.)

Applewood by the River, Aurora (page 42)

Fiddler's Three, Shelbyville (page 135)

Gray Brothers Cafeteria, Mooresville (page 31)

The LaSalle Grill, South Bend (page 121)

Peter's – A Restaurant and Bar, Indianapolis (page 28)

Sahm's Restaurant, Fishers (page 23)

Stone's, Millhousen (page 53)

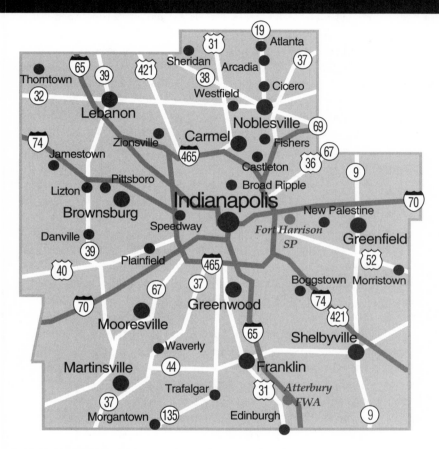

Hoosier heartland throbs with excitement as the cultural and population center of Indiana

Like a giant wheel with radiating spokes formed by seven converging interstate highways, this great pulsing heart of Indiana is in perpetual motion, humming and whirling with the activity of more than a million people.

The central Indiana region offers the recreational and cultural amenities of large metropolitan regions as well as the serenity of lovingly restored historic neighborhoods such as Lockerbie in Indianapolis and charming villages like Zionsville. A multitude of museums, entertainment and sports attractions are clustered in close proximity, and all are easily accessed from downtown Indianapolis where we will begin our journey of the heart.

Some folks with an Indianapolis connection include television show host and comedian David Letterman, news anchor Jane Pauley, basketball legend Oscar Robertson, Grammy-winning songwriter Kenneth "Babyface" Edmonds, composer Noble Sissle, architect Michael Graves and novelists Dan Wakefield and Kurt Vonnegut Jr.

Most first-time visitors are impressed with the extensive construction underway in downtown Indianapolis. New museums, hotels, parks and magnificent sports facilities are a reflection of the economic and cultural vibrancy of this, the nation's twelfth largest city. Appropriately, special attention will be devoted here to "What's New" in Indy.

The development in White River State Park in Downtown Indianapolis of the new national headquarters of the National Collegiate Athletic Association and its Hall of Champions Museum should solidify the city's claim to being "The Amateur Sports Capital of the World." Scheduled to open in March 2000, this architecturally striking facility will offer interactive exhibits and uniquely designed multimedia presentations. It is, however, only one of several new sports-related structures sprouting in Downtown Indianapolis. Also new is the Conseco Fieldhouse, home of the Indiana Pacers. The 1920s retro design of the new home of the Larry Bird-coached NBA team is intended to reflect the proud basketball history in Hoosierland. New since the previous Hometown Restaurants publication is Victory Field, home of the Triple-A Indianapolis Indians. It's regarded as one of the nation's finest ballparks.

As the host of the three largest single-day sporting events in the world, Indianapolis may also stake a claim as the "Racing Capital of the World." The Indianapolis 500-Mile Memorial Day Race, the NASCAR Brickyard 400 in August and the mad dash for the Pole Position on the opening day of qualifications for the Indy 500 draw about one million spectators to the Indianapolis Motor Speedway. Located just northwest of downtown Indianapolis, the 90-year-old, 250,000-seat facility has engines running at a fast pace year round. It's the sound of construction equipment as new race car garages and suites are among improvements added to accommodate the first Formula One United States Grand Prix, scheduled for September 24, 2000. Your visit to the Motor Speedway should include a stop at the Speedway Hall of Fame Museum and a narrated riding tour around the two-and-a-half-mile oval. For details, visit their web site: www.indy500.com.

For a different brand of excitement, we suggest the capital city's Circle Centre shopping and entertainment complex in the heart of the downtown area. Featuring a hundred specialty shops, a multi-screen cinema, nightclubs and an interactive entertainment center, the facility is linked via skywalks to six downtown hotels and the RCA Dome, home of the National Football League's Indianapolis Colts. Some of our favorite shops include Nordstrom's, where efficient service is a religion, and "Back Home Indiana," a shop featuring artwork, books, gourmet food, wines and toys crafted by Indiana artisans. The Abercrombie & Fitch Co. store also is a local favorite. Stroll through the Centre's Artsgarden, a gift of The Lilly Endowment, where exhibits and entertainment provide a pleasant diversion for harried shoppers. Parking is readily available in the sub-street-levels of the facility.

Serious bargain seekers also may wish to visit the sixty-five-store Prime Outlets center at Edinburgh, about a half-hour drive south of Indianapolis via I-65, or the huge Greenwood Mall just off the County Line Road exit of I-65, about ten minutes south of Indianapolis.

Near the Circle Centre is the Indianapolis City Center, 201 S. Capitol Avenue, which offers a great way to plan the remainder of your Indianapolis adventure. Attractions include a free multimedia theatre presentation about the City of Indianapolis, informational brochures on all major attractions and a gift shop. Tours of the RCA Dome may be arranged at the center.

Other new additions to the panoply of visitor opportunities in downtown Indianapolis include the White River Gardens at the Indianapolis Zoo, featuring a dozen themed gardens and the recently expanded Eiteljorg Museum of American Indian and Western Art. Also located in White River State Park is an IMAX theatre and the Indianapolis Zoo. The park also is home to the Congressional Medal of Honor Memorial located on the north bank of the Central Canal. It is the only memorial in the nation that honors all recipients of the Medal of Honor. Dedicated in the summer of 1999, this impressive tribute to America's true heroes includes a touch-screen monitor that provides information about the recipients. The construction of the memorial was sponsored by IPALCO, an Indianapolis-based energy company. Details about the memorial and other White River State Park attractions are available via their web site, www.inwhiteriver.com.

Also opened in the summer of 1999, is the Indiana Historical Society's new 165,000-square-foot headquarters building located at 450 W. Ohio Street on the historic Central Canal. Architecturally stunning, the facility offers visitors fascinating hands-on exhibits, lectures, films and access to the world's largest collection of rare manuscripts, photos and artifacts devoted exclusively to Indiana and the Old Northwest Territory. A restaurant and gift shop also are located in the impressive structure. Closed on Monday, call the society's twenty-four-hour information line for details, (317) 234-1830. The Society's web site is www.indianahistory.org.

Regardless of your age, a visit to the world's largest children's museum should be a part of your itinerary. The Children's Museum and CineDome Theatre, at 30th and Meridian streets, offers five floors of interactive entertainment and enlightenment and is Indiana's top family attraction. The lure of the world's largest water clock and more than 105,000 artifacts draw more than one million visitors annually.

Some other touring tips for the downtown and near-downtown area include:

The Colonel Eli Lilly Civil War Museum located in the basement of the Soldiers and Sailors Monument on Monument Circle, offers interactive displays, battle flags, uniforms and other relics portraying the Hoosier state's extensive involvement in the conflict.

Spectacular views of the city, impressive statuary and the graves of the rich, famous, and notorious will enliven your tour of Crown Hill Cemetery, 700 W. 38th Street, about four miles north of the downtown area. Stop at the 34th Street "Waiting Station" visitor center and pick-up a self-guided tour map. You'll need the map to find your way among the 178,000 interments to the final resting places of Hoosier poet James Whitcomb Riley, bank robber John Dillinger, President Benjamin Harrison and Vice Presidents Thomas R. Marshall, Thomas A. Hendricks, and Charles W. Fairbanks. Eleven Civil War generals and writers Meredith Nicholson and Booth Tarkington also are buried here.

The Indiana State Museum, 202 N. Alabama Street, offers exhibits and other presentations depicting the cultural and natural history of the state. Call (317) 232-1637 for more information.

The Madame C. J. Walker Urban Life Center, located at the triangular corner of Indiana Ave., West and North streets, was built by the woman acclaimed as the nation's first African-American millionaire. Today a restored theatre, exhibitions and other presentations serve to preserve and project the city's rich African-American heritage.

The home of Hoosier Poet James Whitcomb Riley, 528 Lockerbie Street, an Italianate mansion where Riley, author of such treasured poems as "The Old Swimmin' Hole" and "Little Orphant Annie," lived for the twenty years prior to his death in 1916. Now a museum open for tours, exhibits feature Riley's papers and personal belongings and a 1907 player piano. The home is located in the Lockerbie Square Historic District and we suggest a drive through time back to the turn of the century when many of these carefully restored homes were crafted.

Turn-of-the-century retail commerce is the attraction at Hook's 1890 Drug Store on the Indiana State Fairgrounds, 1180 E. 38th Street. One of the nation's largest and most authentic examples of a nineteenth century drug store, antique goods and other drug store memorabilia are on display. Item also may be purchased at the store. Call (317) 927-7500 for more information.

Our prescription for a restful and enlightening interlude is the Indianapolis Museum of Art, 1200 W. 38th Street, located on the 152-acre former estate of members of the pharmaceutical Lilly family. Here you will find "LOVE," the original sculpture by Hoosier artist Robert Indiana. Besides the sculpture garden, features include a nationally acclaimed oriental art collection, a wildlife refuge and a fascinating gift shop. The Garden on the Green restaurant provides road-weary travelers with a pleasant dining atmosphere.

Branching out, visitors will find delightful dining and fascinating visitor attractions in Hamilton County, due north of Indianapolis-Marion County. Prominent among such opportunities is Conner Prairie, 13400 Allisonville Road, in Fishers, where early Northwest Territory and Indiana history comes alive through a museum, a pioneer village and other attractions on the 210-acre site. The open-air living history museum also provides dining and shopping opportunities. Just north of Conner Prairie is the historic county seat, Noblesville, where the Logan Village Shoppes, 977 Logan Street, offer casual shopping at 33 locally owned stores. At nearby Carmel, a unique attraction is the Museum of Miniature Houses, 111 E. Main Street, and an equally unusual dining experience: Illusions Magical Theme Restaurant, 969 Keystone Way, where magicians perform tableside while you dine. Noteworthy among the fine dining establishments in this area is Fletcher's of Atlanta. Chef-owned and operated, the restaurant features unique dishes, many created from local products. Golfers will find fifteen courses, including ones designed by Pete Dye Jr. and Robert Trent Jones, for their fairway fun. For more information on these and other

Hamilton County visitor attractions, call ahead at (800) 776-8687 or visit their web site, www.hccvb.com.

One of the state's most unusual restaurants and more fascinating love stories can be found west of Indianapolis in the Town of Danville. The Mayberry Café is a mecca for fans of *The Andy Griffith Show* and old-fashioned Hoosier home cooking. Memorabilia from the show fills the walls and a television monitor plays continuous episodes of the show. Popular menu items include "Barney's Barbecued Ribs" and "Sheriff Taylor's Prime Rib." Historic homes worthy of note include the Vandegrift Home, south of Danville on State Road 39. A private residence, this brick structure was once the home of Frances "Fanny" Vandegrift who shocked the community by divorcing her husband of twenty-two years and sailing off to Europe in 1875 to study art. It was there she met and fell in love with author and poet Robert Louis Stevenson and, in 1880, became his wife. The famous couple's ashes are buried on a Samoan mountaintop.

Also west of Indianapolis are three of the state's more popular havens for catfish dining fans. Frank and Mary's in Pittsboro, a favorite of former resident and NASCAR driver Jeff Gordon, and Stookey's Restaurant at Thorntown are Central Indiana institutions. Both are in Hendricks County. The Waverly Inn, a Hometown Top Ten selection, is southwest of Indianapolis in Morgan County.

East of Indy, we suggest you complement your tour of the Indianapolis home of poet James Whitcomb Riley with a visit to the Riley Birthplace and Boyhood Home, 250 W. Main Street, Greenfield. Built in 1850, the two-story white frame house is filled with artifacts and other memorabilia of Riley's youth. Carnegie Library fans will delight over lunch at Carnegie's, 100 W. North Street, located in the basement of the restored building.

South of Greenfield, dining in an historic setting is offered in grand style at the Kopper Kettle Restaurant in Morristown. Owned and operated by the same family since 1860, the old Cincinnati-Indianapolis stagecoach inn is filled with antiques, unique stained glass windows and period dinnerware. It's the family style fried chicken dinners that continue to draw travelers from the highway into the elegantly furnished dining rooms of the restaurant.

One of the state's more interesting bed and breakfast facilities is the Rock House at Morgantown. Built in 1894, the exterior of this turreted and gabled Victorian home is embedded with shards of pottery, bits of jewelry, seashells and old photographs.

And, finally, an up-the-downhill ride at Gravity Hill near Mooresville seems to be a fitting way to complete your journey of the Central Heartland. Motorists are amazed at the phenomenon created by stopping their vehicles at the bottom of the hill and watching them coast up for about a quarter of a mile. Local legend has it that the mysterious defiance of gravity is the result of the powers of a Native American witch doctor buried at the foot of the hill.

For more information, call the following local visitors centers:

Indianapolis City Center **800-323-INDY**
Hamilton County Visitors Center **800-321-9666**

ATLANTA

Fletcher's of Atlanta

185 West Main Street, Atlanta, IN 46031
(765) 292-2777

Relax on a train excursion every other week from Fishers to Atlanta to Fletcher's via the Hamiltonian (seasonally), or just enjoy the car ride. In a turn of the century building full of contemporary art, enjoy a "contemporary eclectic menu" packed full of tempting entrees made from locally grown products. Fletcher's, chef-owned and operated, is just "a little bit different." Popular entrees include the Hunan barbecued rack of lamb, and Hog Heaven—bourbon-onion marinated pork chops. Reservations advised.

Open: 5–9 p.m. T–Th, 5–10 p.m. F–S, closed Su–M
MC V

BEECH GROVE

Restaurant nominated by Harry Russell, councilmember

Marty's Morninglory

607 Main St., Beech Grove, IN 46107
(317) 784-1911

Sit back, relax, and visit with your friends over your meal at Marty's Morninglory. The country décor and the friendly staff put you right at ease. Councilmember Russell says his favorite meal at this hometown restaurant is breakfast. Cash only.

Open: 6 a.m.–2 p.m. M–F, 6 a.m.–1 p.m. S, closed Su

Did you know?
Indianapolis is not at the geographic center of the state. Beech Grove stakes that claim.

CARMEL

Restaurant nominated by Norman L. Rundle, councilmember

Chef Rolf's European Café

11588 Westfield Blvd., Carmel, IN 46032
(317) 815-9990

Chef Rolf's marries international cuisine with an intimate, upscale atmosphere and moderate prices, making it a local favorite for business lunches or a nice dinner out. Start your meal with the Magnificent Mushrooms or Fresh Asparagus appetizer, and follow it with one of the international-inspired entrees. The Wednesday-night German buffet is a favorite of Councilman Rundle. Reservations recommended.

Open: 11 a.m.–2:30 p.m. M–F,
5–9:30 p.m. M–Th, 5–10:30 p.m. F, 4–10:30 p.m. S, closed Su
MC V AmEx Di

Did you know?
The first electronic traffic light is believed to have been installed in 1923 in Carmel.

CICERO

Restaurant nominated by Geary Quinn, councilmember

Anvil Inn

29 E. Jackson, Cicero, IN 46034
(317) 984-4533

Antique tools and wood-burning stoves throughout the Anvil Inn pay homage to this 115-year-old building's former position as the town blacksmith business. While the atmosphere gives the Anvil Inn its charm, the steaks, pork chops and catfish satisfy diners' palates. World-famous hashbrowns accent each delicious meal. Relax in the casual tmosphere of the dining room or dine in the cozy bar. Councilmember Quinn recommends the sirloin steak. Weekend reservations recommended. Visit the Inn on the Web at www.anvilinn.com.

Open: 5–9 p.m. W–Th, 5–10 p.m. F–S, closed Su–T
MC V

Jackson Street Café

40 W. Jackson St., Cicero, IN 46034
(317) 984-7137

A state official visited Jackson Street Café recently and enjoyed his meal so much, he later called the town office to declare that he travels all over Indiana and never had tasted such a great grilled tenderloin sandwich and could he have information on moving to Cicero. If that isn't enough of an endorsement, consider the local favorites including the biscuits and gravy breakfast (it's the size of a catcher's mitt!) and the liver and onions lunch special. Cash or check only, please.

Open: 6 a.m.–9 p.m. M–S, closed Su

CLAYTON

Restaurant nominated by Ginny McKamey, clerk-treasurer

Clayton Café

76 E. Kentucky St., Clayton, IN 46118
(317) 539-6419

Clerk-Treasurer McKamey says the catfish at Clayton Café is the best around and is, in fact, her favorite meal here. It's served as the house special on Fridays. Other daily specials and the reasonable prices can't be beat. Cash or check only, please.

Open: 6 a.m.–8 p.m. M–Th, 6 a.m.–9 p.m. F,
6 a.m.–2 p.m. S, closed Su

DANVILLE

Restaurants nominated by Gary D. Eakin, town manager

Dave's All-American Pizza

1247 W. Main St., Danville, IN 46122
(317) 745-6942

Patriotism soars at Dave's, where the interior is a tribute to U.S. veterans. Photos, flags, and other memorabilia adorn the walls, commemorating U.S. military encounters. Over thirty-five items adorn the salad bar, which also features two soups daily. There's also an IU-Purdue room. Dave's is a popular lunch spot. Cash only, please. Sorry, no reservations.

Open: 11 a.m.–2 p.m. T–F, 4:30–9 p.m. T–S, 4:30–9:30 p.m. F–S,
closed Su–M

Mayberry Café

78 W. Main St., Danville, IN 46122
(317) 745-4067

One look at the old sheriff's car outside, and you'll expect to see Barney Fife and Sheriff Andy Taylor seated at the front booth of Mayberry Café. The decor and menu at the restaurant are a tribute to the popular Andy Griffith Show starring Andy Griffith and Don Knotts. Watch reruns of the hit series while you dine. Tuesday night is "Goober's Hat Night," and any customer wearing a hat gets a free dessert with a dinner purchase. Town Manager Eakin says during Indy 500 season, you might get a glimpse of Jim Nabors—a.k.a. Gomer Pyle—who often stops by. Sorry, no reservations.

Open: 11 a.m.–9:30 p.m. Su–Th, 11 a.m.–10 p.m. F–S
MC V

EDINBURGH

Restaurants nominated by Mary Drybread, clerk-treasurer

Bertha's

115 E. Main Cross St., Edinburgh, IN 46124
(812) 526-5249

Chat over coffee or enjoy a delicious home-cooked meal at Bertha's. The homemade pies will make your mouth water. Cash only, please. Sorry, no reservations and no credit cards.

Open: 5 a.m–2:30 p.m. M–F, 5 a.m.–2 p.m. S, closed Su

Roscoe's

129 E. Main Cross St., Edinburgh, IN 46124
(812) 526-6767

Good vegetable soup and pizzas every day except Sunday grace the menu at Roscoe's. You'll notice a replica of the original tin ceiling overhead, while pleasant employees see to your every need. Clerk-Treasurer Drybread suggests the Friday fish special. Sorry, no reservations.

Open: 5 a.m–2 p.m. M–Th & S, 5 a.m.–9 p.m. F,
pizza specials–4:30-9 p.m. Th–F, closed Su

Schaffers Old Towne Inn & Museum

107 E. Main Cross St., Edinburgh, IN 46124
(812) 526-0275

Fine dining and delightful antiques go hand-in-hand at Schaffers. It's been called the most complete antique pharmacy museum in the Midwest. Clerk-Treasurer Drybread says the Christmas buffet is wonderful, but you don't have to wait until the holidays to sample the delicious fare. Reservations accepted.

Open: 11 a.m.–2 p.m. M–F, 5–8 p.m. Th,
5–9 p.m. F–S, closed Su
MC V

Nickel Plate Bar and Grill

8654 E. 116th St., Fishers, IN 46038
(317) 841-2888

Relax and enjoy informal dining at this quaint local pub along the historic Nickel Plate Railroad. Recognized for its giant tenderloin and creative burgers, the Nickel Plate Bar and Grill offers great food and service in a comfortable and friendly atmosphere. Hobo Stew is among the local favorites. Reservations accepted.

Open: 11 a.m.–10 p.m. M–Th, 11 p.m.–midnight F,
11:30–midnight S, 11:30–9 p.m. Su
MC V AmEx Di

Muldoon's

7870 E. 96th St., Fishers, IN 46038
(317) 841-3014

If you're pining away for a glimpse of Ireland, head for Muldoon's straightaway! The casual atmosphere amid the Irish-themed walls would make any true Irishman misty-eyed for the Emerald Isle. Check out the list of domestic and import beers, and consider a tenderloin sandwich.

Open: 11 a.m.–10 p.m. M–Th, 11 a.m.–midnight F–S,
11 a.m–9 p.m. Su
MC V AmEx Di

Sahm's Restaurant

11590 Allisonville Rd., Fishers, IN 46038
(317) 842-1577

The family-owned-and-operated Fishers institution serves local favorites including grilled portobello mushroom and spinach melt sandwiches. As an added benefit, carrot curls are a favorite adornment on the dishes served at Sahm's. The unique menu and the great atmosphere make this restaurant a treat. Check it out on the Web at www.sahms.com.

Open: 11 a.m.–11 p.m. daily
MC V AmEx Di

GREENWOOD

Restaurants nominated by Charles E. Henderson, mayor

Cee J's Bar B-Q

3130 Meridian Parke, Greenwood, IN 46142
(317) 887-1133

Barbecue lovers will want to make sure to stop at Cee J's, where a special sauce makes the barbecued pork stand out. You can dine at the restaurant or carry out your selection.

Open: 11 a.m.–8 p.m. M–S, closed Su
MC V

Oaken Barrel Brewing Company

50 N. Airport Pkwy., Ste. L, Greenwood, IN 46143
(317) 887-2287

You'll find a wide selection of beer and some of the tastiest ribs around in a laid back atmosphere at Oaken Barrel Brewing Company. This casual beer garden has a view of the brewing process. There are 15–20 kinds of beer brewed under one roof. This restaurant is a favorite luncheon meeting site of Mayor Henderson. You can get more information on the Web at www.oakenbarrel.com.

Open: 11:30 a.m.–10p.m. M–Th, 11 a.m.–midnight F,
noon–1 a.m. S, noon–10 p.m. Su
MC V AmEx Di

Restaurant nominated by John M. Gibson, councilmember

Four Seasons Restaurant

1140 N. State Road 135, Greenwood, IN 46142
(317) 859-1985

American specialties intermingled with Greek entrées grace the menu at Four Seasons. A family-dining atmosphere envelops you as you dine on generous portions. Councilman Gibson recommends any of the skillet meals or the roast pork. Sorry, no reservations.

Open: 6 a.m.–10 p.m. daily
MC V AmEx Di

GREENFIELD

China Inn

1274 N. State St., Greenfield, IN
(317) 467-4777

This classic Chinese buffet includes food that is MSG-free. The restaurant specializes in Cantonese, Szechwan, and Hunan, and boasts more than forty items on the buffet. Owners Ying and Yee Zhao, natives of Wu Yi Mountain in China, chose Greenfield to locate their restaurant while looking at a map from their then-Queens, NY, home. General Tso's chicken is a local favorite, and customers also enjoy moo goo gai pan, king crab wrapped with bacon, crab rangoon, dim sum, sweet and sour chicken, and roast pork fried rice.

Open: 11 a.m.–9:30 p.m. T–Th, 11 a.m.–10:30 p.m. F–S,
noon–9:30 p.m. Su, closed M
MC V

Garden House Candies & Eatery

949 N. State St., Greenfield, IN 46140
(317) 462-5244

Step onto the porch of this beautiful older home-turned-restaurant and you'll remember the times you visited your grandparents when you were a child. Pristine hardwood floors covered with small oriental rugs, and antiques to look at, sit on, or buy adorn the restaurant. The aroma of distinctive homemade chocolates will draw you to the creams, tiger butter, turtles, chocolate-covered Oreos, and other homemade confections. The menu contains many soups, sandwiches, salads, and of course, homemade desserts to choose from. Cash or checks only please.

Open: 11 a.m.–3 p.m. M–F
by reservation only S–Su & evenings

Restaurant nominated by Marilyn Levering, councilmember

Carnegie's

100 W. North St., Greenfield, IN 46140
(317) 462-8480

Elegant dining is alive and well in Greenfield in the basement of the old public library building. Let Carnegie's proprietor and chef Ian Harrison delight you with his creations. Try the Five Lilies Soup and the Ravioli of Spinach and Ricotta. Councilmember Levering also recommends the grilled salmon. Reservations recommended on weekends.

Open: 11 a.m.–1:30 p.m. T–F (lunch), 5–9 p.m. T–S (dinner)
MC V Di

INDIANAPOLIS

Fireside South

522 E. Raymond St., Indianapolis, IN 46203
(317) 788-4521

For 46 years folks have been coming from all over to enjoy the great steaks and authentic tasting German food at Fireside South. Private dining areas make it a popular spot for group parties. The filet comes highly recommended as well. Carry-out is available. Reservations advised.

Open: 11 a.m.–10 p.m. M–Th, 11 a.m.–11 p.m. F, 4–11 p.m. S,
closed Su
MC V AmEx Di

Joe's Shelby Street Diner

3623 Shelby Street, Indianapolis, IN 46227
(317) 783-9590

The claim to fame at Joe's is the largest hamburger and the largest BLT in Indianapolis. The burgers are a full pound and a pound of bacon adorns the BLT. It's a fun '50s-style diner where the burgers, fries and shakes will take you back to yesteryear. Cash only, please.

Open: 7 a.m.–8 p.m. M–Th, 7 a.m.–9 p.m. F–S, closed Su

Restaurant nominated by Charles E. Henderson, mayor, Greenwood

Shallos

8811 S. Hardegan, Indianapolis, IN 46227
(317) 882-7997

Beer connoisseurs will want to make a beeline for Shallos, self-proclaimed "purveyors of rare and exotic beers." There are 500 kinds of the brew featured at this Southside establishment, which also offers a house specialty of a homemade chips & dip appetizer plus delicious sandwiches and entrées. Reservations accepted for parties of 10 or more. Call-ahead seating is available.

Open: 11 a.m.–midnight M–Th, 11 a.m.–1 a.m. F–S,
11 a.m.–10 p.m. Su
MC V AmEx Di

Restaurants nominated by Georgia Stevens, councilmember, Greenwood

Chanteclair

2501 S. High School Road, Indianapolis, IN 46241
(317) 243-1040

If you're looking for a place to celebrate a special occasion or just want to enjoy an elegant dinner, try Chanteclair. The service is outstanding and the food is memorable. Councilmember Stevens suggests the New York strip. Reservations recommended.

Open: 5:30–10:30 p.m. M–S, closed Su
MC V AmEx Di

Peter's – A Restaurant and Bar

8505 Keystone Crossing, Indianapolis, IN 46240
(317) 465-1155

In an area of Indianapolis ripe with fine restaurants, Peter's stands out as one of the classics. You'll dine on delicious food in an upscale environment, such as Chef Dave's signature salad and seared-to-rare tuna. Their New York strip is among the best in town, and the desserts are out of this world. Reservations required.

Open: 5–10 p.m. M–Th, 5–10:30 p.m. F–S, closed Su
MC V DC

Restaurant nominated by John M. Gibson, councilmember, Greenwood

Paragon Restaurant

118 S. Girls School Rd., Indianapolis, IN 46231
(317) 271-3514

Choose from Greek, Italian, or American offerings at Paragon, where the food is served piping hot. A friendly staff highlights your experience in a casual atmosphere. You'll find a lot to choose from as you consider the breakfast, lunch or dinner specials.

Open: 6 a.m.–midnight daily
MC V AmEx Di

Did you know?
Indianapolis is both a consolidated city (with Marion County) and the state's only city of the first class.

JAMESTOWN

Restaurant nominated by Todd Thompson, councilmember, Lizton

B&B Tavern and Grill

34 E. Main St., Jamestown, IN
(765) 676-5298

Hometown pride is strong at the B&B, where servers pride themselves on fast, friendly service. Play a relaxing game of pool before your meal. Councilmember Thompson recommends any steak or the Cajun chicken and Cajun fries. Sorry, no reservations.

Open: 11 a.m.–10 p.m. M–S, 11 a.m.–9 p.m. Su
MC V

MARTINSVILLE

Restaurants nominated by Shannon Buskirk, mayor,
and Harold Stanger, councilmember

Forkey's

539 E. Morgan, Martinsville, IN 46151
(765) 342-2033

Seasonal decorations are a feast for your eyes as much as the menu is a treat for your tastebuds at Forkey's. You won't find a cleaner dining establishment or friendlier staff. They're proud of their catfish and homemade biscuits and gravy. Mayor Buskirk recommends the pan-fried tenderloin and the weekend breakfast buffet. Cash or check only. Reservations available.

Open: 6 a.m.–2 p.m. M–W, 6 a.m.–8 p.m. Th–F, 6 a.m.–2 p.m. S, 7
a.m.–2 p.m. Su

Did you know?
The first successful goldfish farm in the nation was founded at Martinsville in 1899 by Eugene Curtis Shireman with two hundred fish. Today, it still ranks among the biggest goldfish producers in the world.

McCORDSVILLE

Restaurant nominated by Cheryl Stoner, deputy clerk-treasurer

Casio's

6765 W. Pendleton Pike, McCordsville, IN 46055
(317) 335-2237

The '20s and '30s come alive at Casio's, where the history is as intriguing as the food is delicious. Legend has it that John Dillinger escaped through the office door of the former gambling casino with the FBI in hot pursuit. If you ask, the staff will give you a guided tour of the historic Art Deco building, including the bulletproof cashier's room. Keep your eyes open for "The Blue Lady," Casio's ghost who travels in a blue mist on cold nights. Reservations advised.

Open: 5:30–10 p.m. T–Th, 5:30–11 p.m. F–S;
lounge open 3 p.m.–closing M–S; closed Su
MC V Di

MOORESVILLE

Restaurant nominated by councilmembers Toby Dolen and Robert Wooden, Monrovia

Gray Brothers Cafeteria

555 S. Indiana St., Mooresville, IN 46158
(317) 831-3345

Faithful patrons come from all around to enjoy the superb food at Gray Brothers. Be sure to bring your appetite—the wide variety of food means making a decision can be difficult. And you'll want to leave room for a piece of homemade pie. Sorry, no reservations.

Open: 11 a.m.–9 p.m. daily
MC V AmEx Di

MORGANTOWN

Kathy's

159 W. Washington, Morgantown, IN 46160
(812) 597-2729

The home-style cooking at Kathy's is outdone only by the delicious pies from which diners may choose. Councilmember Stanger says you can't go wrong with anything on the menu. "The food is like home cooking, it's great," Stanger says. Cash or check only.

Open: 7:30 a.m.–7 p.m. M–W & F–S, closed Th & Su

MORRISTOWN

Restaurants nominated by Joe Neeb, town manager

Kopper Kettle Inn

135 W. Main St., Morristown, IN 46161
(765) 763-6767

Unique antiques from the serving dishes to stained glass windows adorn each room of the turn-of-the-century Kopper Kettle Inn, a historic stop on the old Indianapolis-Cincinnati stagecoach line. Visitors from all over have journeyed to this local favorite to taste the fried chicken, Town Manager Neeb's favorite. Reservations accepted.

Open: 11 a.m.–8:30 p.m. T–S, 11:30 a.m.–6:30 p.m. Su, closed M
MC V AmEx Di

Bluebird Restaurant

158 E. Main St., Morristown, IN 46161
(765) 763-7155

Folks like to catch up on all the local news at the Bluebird's round table while enjoying some of the hometown favorites such as roast beef Manhattan and fried chicken. Feel free to pull up a chair!

Open: 6 a.m.–8 p.m. M–S, 6 a.m.–2 p.m. Su
MC V Di

NORTH SALEM

Restaurant nominated by Todd Thompson, councilmember, Lizton

Red Dog Steakhouse and Saloon

8 W. Pearl St., North Salem, IN 46165
(765) 676-6217

After a day of antique hunting, stop by the Red Dog Steakhouse and Saloon for a memorable hometown meal. Browse in the four antique shops nearby, then stop in for a tender applewood-cooked steak. The Red Dog is located just 25 miles west of Indy off I-74. Reservations recommended.

Open: 3–11 p.m. M, 10 a.m.–10 p.m. T–S, closed Su
MC V

PITTSBORO

Restaurant nominated by Todd Thompson, councilmember, Lizton

Frank and Mary's

21 E. Main St., Pittsboro, IN 46167
(317) 892-3485

An occasional hangout for Indianapolis Motor Speedway celebrities, Frank and Mary's is one of Hoosierland's more famous catfish dinner spots. With over 40 years of ownership by the same family, hometown pride is alive and well at Frank and Mary's. The owners, proud of Pittsboro's own NASCAR driver Jeff Gordon, have adorned the restaurant and bar with racing memorabilia. Come and enjoy the atmosphere. Reservations accepted for parties of 10 or more.

Open: 11 a.m.–2 p.m. & 5–10 p.m. M–Th,
11 a.m.–10 p.m. F–S, closed Su
MC V Di

SHELBYVILLE

Restaurants nominated by Betsy Stephen, mayor

Compton's Cow Palace

318 N. Harrison St., Shelbyville, IN 46176
(317) 392-4889

Known for its marvelous selection of ice cream, Compton's Cow Palace uses an old-fashioned Purdue University formula in its products, which are made locally in its Shelbyville ice cream plant down the street. Delicious breakfast, lunch and dinner specials are a tasty precursor to the real treat — the ice cream! Mayor Stephen recommends the blueberry pancakes or garden omelet. Or try a fun ice cream-inspired breakfast treat like peanut butter fudge pancakes (Reeses pieces pancake topped with vanilla ice cream, hot fudge and warm peanut butter). The lunches and dinners are a taste treat too! An ATM machine is available at this cash-only restaurant.

Open: 6 a.m.–9 p.m. M–S, 8 a.m.–9 p.m. Su
(breakfast served until 10:30 a.m. M–F, 11:30 a.m. S–Su)

Chicken Inn

541 E. Hendricks St., Shelbyville, IN 46176
(317) 392-6088

As the name suggests, chicken is the specialty of the house at Chicken Inn, particularly the broasted chicken. The locals will tell you, though, that the burgers and other menu items are good, too. Mayor Stephen suggests the fried chicken with green beans, mashed potatoes and gravy, and slaw. Or try a Big Joy (an old-fashioned double-decker burger) and a side of Homer's (homemade onion rings). Dine in or carry out. Cash only.

Open: 11 a.m.–8:30 p.m. T–Th, 11 a.m.–9 p.m. F–S,
11 a.m.–2 p.m. Su, closed M

Hamilton House

132 W. Washington St., Shelbyville, IN 46176
(317) 392-1350

You'll find fine dining in a historic setting at the Hamilton House, a two-story restored Victorian home listed on the National Register of Historic Places. The menu is upscale; the prices are anything but. Try the Lemon Peppered Salmon or the Honey Grilled Rack of Pork. The dessert menu features such offerings as Mimi's Sugar Cream Pie, Hummingbird Cake and Brownstone Front Cake. For a lighter bite, both Mayor Stephen and Councilmember Roland Stine recommend the chicken salad, which includes sweetbread and fruit pudding. Reservations preferred.

Open: 11 a.m.–2 p.m. & 5–9 p.m. T–S, 11 a.m–3 p.m. Su, closed M
MC V AmEx Di

Restaurant nominated by James Garrett, councilmember

Fiddler's Three

1415 E. Michigan Rd., Shelbyville, IN 46176
(317) 392-4371

Dine alfresco on the patio or enjoy the light playing through the beautiful leaded glass windows enhancing the atmosphere at Fiddler's Three, where you'll find some of the best steaks around. Councilmember Garrett recommends the chicken Cordon Bleu or prime rib. Be sure to check out the nightly specials. Reservations advised.

Open: 5–9 p.m. T–S, closed Su–M
MC V

Did you know?
Thomas Edison was once a Western Union telegraph operator at Union Station in Indianapolis.

SOUTHPORT

Restaurant nominated by Nannette Tunget, mayor

Courtyard Café

2028 E. Southport Rd., Southport, IN 46227
(317) 786-8583

Located on the south side of Indianapolis you can find a gem of a restaurant where Cajun and Creole dishes dazzle your tastebuds and the desserts are heavenly. Relax in the courtyard setting amid a soft glow from street lamps while the fountain trickles in the background. If New Orleans-style food isn't your cup of tea, Mayor Tunget suggests the tuna melt or the Courtyard Chicken Salad. Plan to allow time to visit the Southport Antique Mall, which is directly in front of the Courtyard Café. Reservations for large parties are advised.

Open: 11 a.m.–7 p.m. M–S, closed Su
MC V AmEx

THORNTOWN

Restaurant nominated by Dale Dickerson, councilmember

Stookey's Restaurant

125 E. Main St., Thorntown, IN 47061
(765) 436-7202

Catfish, ribeye, onion rings, and homemade vinegar slaw are the trademarks at Stookey's, according to Councilman Dickerson, who says the hot food is served hot, and the cold food is served cold. If in doubt about your meal, go with the catfish. It always gets the checkered flag. A racing theme highlights the interior. Sorry, no reservations.

Open: 11 a.m.–2 p.m. M–S, 5–9 p.m. T–Th, 5–10 p.m. F–S
MC V AmEx Di

SOUTH CENTRAL

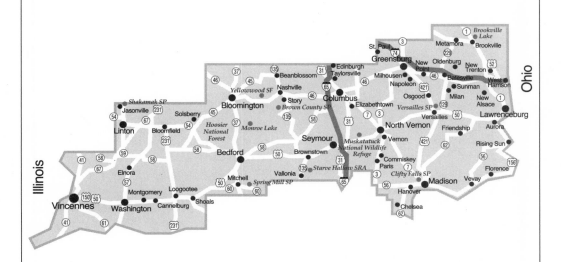

Begin with revolution and find peace in the precious past and scenic sites of Indiana's South Central Region

From the many historic sites in the west at Vincennes, including an American Revolutionary War battle site, to the glitter and excitement of riverboat gaming in the east, the South Central region offers a cornucopia of diverse opportunities for tourism.

Some of the world's most renowned architects have designed a stunning array of modern structures at Columbus on the prairie while preservationists have created a complement in the charming historic architecture of Madison on the Ohio River.

The cosmopolitan university community of Bloomington's appeal finds a counterpart in the charm of the restored canal era town of Metamora.

One of the state's most scenic drives along the Ohio River, from Madison to Lawrenceburg, is matched by the "Mile of History" tour at Vincennes.

Wherever you visit off the major highways in this region you may expect to find friendly people, less clutter, a slower pace and attractions with short lines and smiling faces to greet you.

Getting around in the South Central Region is a breeze with U.S. 50 slicing east-west through the region and Interstates 65 and 74 providing north-south access in the east. U.S. 41 and U.S. 231 and Indiana State Road 37 provide good north-south passage in the west section.

Your starting point should be where your heart and taste buds direct you, but we'll suggest a route across the region, beginning in historic Vincennes. This tour will steer us through Washington, Montgomery, Bedford, Bloomington, Columbus, Madison, and Lawrenceburg. From Lawrenceburg we'll suggest an extension through Milan to Batesville, Oldenburg, and Metamora.

Founded in 1732, Vincennes is Indiana's oldest city and, thankfully, much of its history has been preserved. Highlights of your tour should include the George Rogers Clark National Historic Park, 401 S. 2nd Street. Located on twenty-six acres at the site of old Fort Sackville, it is a shrine to Lieutenant Colonel George Rogers Clark and his frontier army, which marched in mid-winter from Kaskaskia on the Mississippi to defeat the British here on February 25, 1779. Within walking distance is Grouseland, the home of Indiana Territory Governor William Henry Harrison from 1804–1812. Harrison, later to become the ninth President of the United States, often negotiated treaties on the front lawn of the home with the tribal leaders of Native Americans, including the famous chief Tecumseh. Later, Harrison was to defeat both Tecumseh and his brother, the Prophet, in battles. A stop at the Log Cabin Visitor Center at the corner of Harrison and Park streets is recommended to obtain maps and other information on the many historic homes and businesses in Vincennes. Fans of the late Red Skelton will want to see the comedian's birthplace at 111 Lyndale Avenue. Skelton lived there until he was twelve, when he left to join a traveling medicine show.

Moving east on U.S. 50 to Washington, we suggest a visit to the Daviess County Historical Society Museum located in a two-story red brick schoolhouse on Donaldson Road south of the city. The museum includes fifteen rooms of exhibitions and collections. Call (812) 254-5122 for details.

About seven miles east of Washington stop at Montgomery. Just north of town is the Gasthof restaurant, bakery, gift shop and village, where the crafts and cuisine reflect the traditions and tastes of this Amish region.

Continuing east on U.S. 50 we will exit about one and a half miles east of Huron to take State Road 60 to Mitchell, home of Virgil I. "Gus" Grissom, one of the nation's seven original astronauts. A limestone memorial to Grissom which stands forty-four feet high is located at city hall, four blocks south of Main Street on South Sixth Street.

From Mitchell, head north on State Road 37 to Bloomington. It's four-lane most of the way and provides some breathtaking views of Indiana's Limestone Country.

Bloomington, film site of the movie *Breaking Away*, offers diverse doses of art, music, a lively nightlife, sports and Indiana's only Tibetan Cultural Center. A good place to start is to call the Bloomington Convention and Visitors Bureau, (800) 800-0037 or visit their web site, www.visitbloomington.com. You may be overwhelmed to find numerous art and craft galleries, museums and many other fascinating diversions in Bloomington, so we'll make a few suggestions. A must stop is the Fine Arts Plaza on E. 7th Street and the Indiana University Art Museum and the Lilly Library. Paintings by Monet and Picasso are among more than 35,000 objects on display at the museum, designed by the world-renowned architectural firm of I. M. Pei and Partners. The Gutenburg and Coverdale bibles and John James Audubon's *Birds of America* prints are among more than 400,000 books, six million manuscripts and 130,000 pieces of sheet music housed at the library. We also suggest a visit to the Oliver Winery facility north of Bloomington at 8024 N. State Road 37. Indiana's oldest and largest winery, distinctive limestone sculptures reminiscent of England's Stone Hendge greet visitors to a huge wine-tasting room and gift shop. The fifteen-acre facility is open year-round and offers free wine tasting daily. Oliver produces fifteen premium wines, including our favorite, Camelot Mead, a honey wine. Outdoor decks and a small pond on the property provide ideal wine-and-cheese picnic sites. Call (812) 876-5800 for details.

From Bloomington, head east on State Road 46 about 8 miles to Belmont and turn south on Steele Road for about one and a half miles to the T. C. Steele State Historic Site where the eleven-room House of the Singing Winds is the centerpiece of a true hidden Hoosier Treasure. Steele (1847–1926) is considered Indiana's most famous representational artist. Located on a hilltop overlooking acres of gardens, lily ponds, nature preserves and hiking trails, the 211-acre retreat is an appropriate tribute to the Indiana impressionist artist. Behind the house is the artist's studio with a changing display of his paintings.

Back to State Road 46, head east about eight miles to the artist colony of Nashville. If it's time to bed down, we recommend the charming Artists Colony Inn on Main Street. The twenty-three-room clapboard hostelry doubles as an art gallery with paintings and other artwork gracing the walls and other public areas. Indeed, the inn boasts its own artist in residence, Frederick Rigley. The rates are reasonable and the bonus is the excellent food served at the inn's restaurant. Our luncheon favorite there is Lucie's Pot Pie with a side of Beef Barley Soup. The inn is at the center of a pleasant array of shops, restaurants and galleries that feature the work of more than a hundred local artists. Call (800) 737-0255 for additional information.

Motoring east from Nashville on State Road 46 about eighteen miles you will find the Athens of the Prairie, Columbus, known worldwide for its contemporary architecture. First stop is the Visitors Center, 506 Fifth Street, to obtain information on architectural tours and lodging. If you prefer unique lodging, we suggest the Columbus Inn, 445 Fifth Street, a luxury bed-and-breakfast hotel located in the 1895 neo-Romanesque City Hall, considered one of the top ten of its kind in the nation.

Saying, Goodbye, Columbus, we'll head southeast on State Road 7 to the Ohio River community of Madison, where the restoration of the city's historic homes and other structures is in high gear in the state's largest historic district. Noteworthy among the attractions is the Lanier Mansion State Historic Site and its famous spiral staircase, undergoing restoration to return it to its 1840s splendor. Historians treat its occupant,

James F. D. Lanier, with fondness because he provided financing for Indiana's Civil War debts in an amount totaling more than $1 million. Here, too, you will find Indiana's oldest volunteer fire fighter's headquarters, The Fair Play Fire Company No. 1, at 403 E. Main Street. The Jeremiah Sullivan House, 304 W. Second Street, dates to 1818. Sullivan is credited with naming the city of Indianapolis and, ironically, a grandson and a great-grandson became mayors of the capital city.

Now, we'll venture east via scenic State Road 56, which hugs the Ohio River. Several charming communities grace the Ohio River shores on this scenic drive. These include the Swiss-settled Vevay where the Switzerland County Historical Museum at E. Main and Market streets, offers visitors a glimpse into the community's past and a look at what is believed to be the first piano brought to Indiana. At Rising Sun you'll find historic buildings and a modern day wonder, The Grand Victoria Hotel and Casino. The Ohio County Historical Museum, 218 S. Walnut Street, is undergoing major renovation. A former plow factory, the museum houses several wonders including Hoosier Boy, a racing boat of the 1920s era which still holds the speed record from Cincinnati to Louisville on the Ohio River. Also on display is Indiana's first electric chair. Now, on to Aurora where the fine dining is topped only by the lofty Hillforest Mansion. This "Steamboat Gothic" home features circular porches, columns and a round cupola resembling the pilot house of an old Steamboat. The home sets majestically atop a hill overlooking the city. Completed in 1856 features also include twin bay windows, iron fireplace mantels, walnut parquet floors and porcelain keyhole covers. On a clear day, the front porch affords visitors a spectacular view of parts of three states, Indiana, Ohio and Kentucky. Heading about a mile east to Lawrenceburg, motorists will view numerous roadside enticements to spend time and money at the Argosy Casino and Hotel, billed as the nation's most visited riverboat/casino.

Our final leg of the journey includes Milan, Batesville, Oldenburg and Metamora, where a full plate of early southeast Indiana history can be savored. About fifteen miles northwest of Aurora via State Road 350 is Milan, a town which serves as a perpetual shrine to the state's most revered activity, high school basketball. It was from this town in 1954 that the 161-student Milan High School ventured forth to win the state high school basketball championship. The miraculous feat was captured forever in the movie, "Hoosiers." Memorabilia of the event can be seen at the Milan Railroad Inn restaurant on East Carr St. Now head north on State Road 101 about ten miles and west on State Road 46 about six miles to Batesville. This charming community is home to the Hillenbrand-owned furniture, casket and related industries. The Hillenbrand family pioneered Indiana furniture making, beginning in the 1870s and is now the principal employer in the region. A recommended stop is the Sherman House at Main and George streets, where diners are treated to German specialty dishes and the ambiance of an old Vienna café.

Taking State Road 229 about three miles north of Batesville you will find the Village of Spires, Oldenburg, home of the Immaculate Conception Convent of the Sisters of St. Francis as well as a former Franciscan Monastery. Historic chapels, churches and a grotto dot the central section of the town. Founded in 1817, the community's architecture and tastes reflects the German Catholic influence of its early settlers. Other reminders of its

German heritage can be found on the tempting menu at the Brau Haus as well as the restaurant's address on "Wasserstrasse." You can't go wrong with the fried chicken dinner or the reasonable prices at the Brau Haus or the nearby Wagner's Village Inn. As you head north on State Road 229 toward U.S. 52 and Metamora, look for the "Sisters' Cow Barn" on your right on the outskirts of Oldenburg. Once used by the Sisters of St. Francis, the barn is believed to be the largest in the country. After eleven miles you should find Old Metamora, named after a fictional Native American princess. The original Metamora was a main stop on the Whitewater Canal and is now preserved as The Whitewater Canal State Historic Site, featuring specialty shops, railroad and canal rides and great food. Among the more popular attractions is the Metamora Grist and Roller Mill. Located by an old canal lock, the facility continues to function as a gristmill and museum. And, you may purchase a bag of the cornmeal as it emerges from the mill. A half-hour ride on the horse-drawn canal boat, the Ben Franklin, heightens the understanding of the mid-1800s when this mode of transportation was popular. We suggest you complete your day with a fried chicken dinner at the Hearthstone Restaurant on U.S. 52, where scenes from the 1988 hit movie *Rainman* were filmed.

There is, of course, much more to see and do in the beautiful and bountiful area of Indiana. Too, there are numerous great dining opportunities in the pages to follow. And hundreds of folks are anxious to help you plan your journey.

For more information, call one of the visitors centers listed below:

Bloomington/Monroe County .... (800) 800-0037
Columbus Visitors Center .... (812) 378-2622
Dearborn County .... (800) 322-8198
Jennings County .... (800) 928-3667
Madison Visitors Bureau .... (800) 559-2956
Nashville/Brown County .... (800) 365-7327
Metamora .... (765) 647-2109

AURORA

Restaurants nominated by Richard Ullrich, clerk-treasurer

Applewood by the River

215 Judiciary St., Aurora, IN 47001
(812) 926-1166

You'll find everything from pork chops to meatloaf to filet mignon at Applewood by the River, located in the historic Odd Fellows Hall. In addition to the delectable dining, feast your eyes on a scenic view of the Ohio River. Weekend reservations recommended.

Open: 11 a.m.–10 p.m. M–Th, 11 a.m.–11 p.m. F–S,
11 a.m.–10 p.m. Su
MC V AmEx Di

Coachlight Inn

223 Third St., Aurora, IN 47001
(812) 926-4006

The historic Pelgen's Hotel is home to the Coachlight Inn, where visitors are greeted with an array of antiques including a hundred-year-old bar and an antique player piano. Then, you can treat your tastebuds with all sorts of treats. The pot roast over buttered noodles or the Bar-B-Q baby back ribs are outstanding. Be sure to save room for the outstanding dessert selection. Reservations available.

Open: 7 a.m.–11 p.m. daily
MC V AmEx Di

Did you know?
The Empire State Building, Rockefeller Center, Grand Central Station, the *Chicago Tribune* Tower, the Waldorf Astoria Hotel, the Indiana State Capitol, and the Chicago Museum of Science and Industry were all built with Indiana limestone.

BATESVILLE

Cricket Ridge Public Restaurant/Golf Course

22087 Pocket Rd., Batesville, IN 47006
(812) 933-0414

Good food and good service is what you will experience at Cricket Ridge. After a long day of golf, relax in a casual atmosphere on the deck overlooking the water. The daily luncheon specials are out of this world — especially the grilled chicken breast. The breaded or grilled tenderloins are also something to experience. On Fridays and Saturdays, try the prime rib. Small party room available. Reservations accepted.

Open: 10:30 a.m.–9 p.m. M–Th, 10:30 a.m.–10 p.m. F–S,
10:30 a.m.–8 p.m. Su
MC V Di

BLOOMINGTON

Restaurants nominated by John Fernandez, mayor

The Irish Lion

212 W. Fifth St., Bloomington, IN 47401
(812) 336-9076

A classic Irish pub setting is what you'll find at The Irish Lion, along with great music from the Emerald Isle and yards of beer. Try the Blarney puff balls for an appetizer, or any of the authentic Irish dishes. The salmon is a favorite of Mayor Fernandez.

Open: 11 a.m.–3 a.m. M–S, 11 a.m.–midnight Su
MC V AmEx Di

Ladyman's Café

122 E. Kirkwood Ave., Bloomington, IN 47408
(812) 336-5557

Ladyman's has been a staple on Bloomington's square for fifty years. The locals love the classic Hoosier diner where you can't go wrong with the special of the day. Cash only. Sorry, no reservations.

Open: 6 a.m.–5:30 p.m. M–S, 7:30 a.m.–4 p.m. Su

Michael's Uptown Café

102 E. Kirkwood Ave., Bloomington, IN 47408
(812) 339-0900

Mayor Fernandez heads for Michael's Uptown Café when he's in the mood for Cajun porkchops. The paintings adorning the walls are a treat for your eyes, too. Relax with a fine meal in a casual atmosphere.

Open: 7 a.m.–10 p.m. M–S, 9 a.m.–2 p.m. Su
MC V AmEx Di

COLUMBUS

The Ribeye Steak and Ribs

2506 25th St., Columbus, IN 47201
(812) 376-6410

The fresh cut steaks and a "super" salad bar are what has made The Ribeye Steak and Ribs a popular attraction for local officials and visitors from around Indiana for over 25 years. Don't miss out on the fresh-baked bread and cheesecake. There's also a full bar on-site. Reservations accepted.

Open: 11 a.m.–1:30 p.m. M–F, 5–9 p.m. M–Th,
5–10 p.m. F, 4–10 p.m. S, closed Su
MC V AmEx Di

CROTHERSVILLE

Restaurant nominated by Nancy Nay, clerk-treasurer

Walnut Street Inn

104 E. Walnut St., Crothersville, IN 47229
(812) 793-2944

A circa-1917 home is the site of one of Crothersville's newest dining establishments. Different rooms in the house offer diners a choice of atmosphere, while the menu provides an ample array of entrées for diners to choose from. Clerk-Treasurer Nay recommends the caribou winter stew. Reservations accepted.

Open: 11 a.m.–8 p.m. M–S, 11 a.m.–2 p.m. Su
MC V

GREENSBURG

Restaurants nominated by Frank Manus, mayor

Cattlemen's Inn

1703 N. Lincoln, Greensburg, IN 47240
(812) 663-2411

Affordable prices and a great lunch and dinner buffet make Cattlemen's Inn a favorite of Mayor Manus. He recommends the broasted chicken. A dazzling Sunday buffet offers a weekend treat.

Open: 11 a.m.–10 p.m. M–Th, 11 a.m.–11 p.m. F–S,
11 a.m.–8 p.m. Su
MC V AmEx

Heritage Acres

5084 W. Old Highway 46, Greensburg, IN 47240
(812) 663-1088 or (888) 663-1088

Work up an appetite before heading to Heritage Acres. You'll need a reservation for the all-you-can-eat family-style meal and you'll want to savor every bite. Be sure to save room for some hot fudge cobbler. Breakfast, lunch, and dinner by reservation only. No credit cards.

Open by reservation only T–Su

Stories Restaurant

109 E. Main St., Greensburg, IN 47240
(812) 663-9948

After you check out the famous Tower Trees growing on the roof of the courthouse in Greensburg head across the street to Stories, where you can enjoy Mayor Manus' favorites, the fried chicken and hand-breaded tenderloins. His Honor says it's no tall tale that the service is first-rate and the homemade pies will "melt in your mouth."

Open: 8 a.m.–7:30 p.m. M–S, closed Su
MC V

HOPE

Restaurants nominated by Shirley Robertson, clerk-treasurer

The Filling Station

525 S. Main St., Hope, IN 47246
(812) 546-5727

Large round tables invite diners to share their mealtime at The Filling Station. Browse the country crafts for sale while you wait for your food. Clerk-Treasurer Robertson recommends the ham or Swiss steak dinner and a Sarah salad. Cash or check only, please. Group reservations available.

Open: 7 a.m.–8 p.m. M–S, 7 a.m.–4 p.m. Su

Ron's Broasted Chicken

704 N.Main St., Hope, IN 47246
(812) 546-0444

Breaded tenderloin sandwiches and chicken tenders highlight the menu at Ron's. The seating is limited, but you can ask for carry-out and take it to the nearby Hope Town Square Park for a picnic. Sorry, no reservations.

Open: 5 a.m.–9 p.m. M–F, 6 a.m.–9 p.m. S,
11 a.m.–9 p.m. Su
MC V AmEx Di

JASONVILLE

Restaurants nominated by Charlotte Thomas, clerk-treasurer

Shakamak Family Restaurant

121 W. Main St., Jasonville, IN 47438
(812) 665-2154

Hand-sawed logs grace the interior of the Shakamak Family Restaurant, lending a rustic touch to a restaurant named for nearby Shakamak State Park. Clerk-Treasurer Thomas' favorite meal consists of sliced beef, mashed potatoes and gravy, vegetable soup, and homemade rolls. Cash only. Reservations accepted.

Open: 5:30 a.m.–9:30 p.m. daily

Sharon's Kountry Kitchen

101 E. Main St., Jasonville, IN 47438
(812) 665-4177

Shakamak State Park and Hillenbrand Fish and Wildlife Area offer the perfect setting for Sharon's, where you'll not only taste delicious food but you'll get a taste of the heritage and culture of southwestern Indiana. You'll want to try the BBQ baby back ribs or smoked chicken at "the best-kept secret in Greene County." A number of specialty sandwiches and daily specials also grace the menu.

Open: 5:30 a.m.–9 p.m. M–S, 5:30 a.m.–2 p.m. Su
MC V AmEx Di

LAWRENCEBURG

Whiskey's Historic Family Restaurant

334 Front St., Lawrenceburg, IN 47025
(812) 537-4239

Located in a city that boasts two of the nation's largest distilleries, Seagram's and Schenley, you can trust that Whiskey's Historic Family Restaurant serves only the best food and drink. After you work up an appetite by touring the distilleries, you will want to try the delicious cod fish dinner, that is if you still have room after savoring the barbecued potato skins as an appetizer. The smoked ribs and steaks are good, too. Reservations accepted.

Open: 11:30 a.m.–10 p.m. M–F, 4–11 p.m. S, closed Su
MC V AmEx Di

LINTON

Restaurant nominated by Charlotte Thomas, clerk-treasurer, Jasonville.

Stoll's Country Inn

Highway 54, Linton, IN 47441
(812) 847-2477

Jasonville Clerk-Treasurer Thomas likes to travel to Stoll's to savor the delicious Amish home-style cooking and the friendly atmosphere. Every dish is made from scratch at this hometown favorite, and the Friday night seafood buffet is sure to please. Sorry, no reservations.

Open: 7 a.m.–8 p.m.M–Th, 7 a.m.–9 p.m. F–S, closed Su
MC V AmEx Di

The Grill

269 A Street NE, Linton, IN 47441
(812) 847-9010

You're in mining country when you're in Linton. You'll enjoy learning about the area's rich coal mining heritage by browsing around the interior of The Grill. Take a good look at the display of coal mining photographs. If you have a miner's appetite, try the tenderloin and fries. Visit on weekends for grilled-out steaks, prepared by the owner, himself. Breakfast is served anytime. Sorry, no reservations and no credit cards.

Open: 5 a.m.–7 p.m. M–Th, 5 a.m.–8 p.m. F–S, 5 a.m.–2 p.m. Su

LOOGOOTEE

Restaurants nominated by Bill Parker, mayor

The Cabin

US 231 at Williams St., Loogootee, IN 47553
(812) 295-9475

It's a toss-up as to whether the home cooking or the tall tales at the "liars table" draw local diners to The Cabin. Regardless, Mayor Parker recommends the grilled chicken sandwich . . . and that's the truth! Cash only, please.

Open: 5 a.m.–8 p.m. T–S, 5 a.m.–3 p.m. Su, closed M

Lakeview

U.S. 231 N, Loogootee, IN 47553
(812) 295-3299

Seafood and catfish highlight the buffet every Friday at Lakeview, where the Amish cooking is sensational and the atmosphere will make you feel right at home. Reservations accepted for parties of six or more.

Open: 6 a.m.–9 p.m. M–S, closed Su
MC V AmEx Di

MADISON

Note: For more details on these Madison restaurants visit www.oldmadison.com.

OVO Café

209 W. Main St., Madison, IN 47250
(812) 273-8808

Sophisticated continental cuisine meets small town America at OVO Café. A unique Kentucky hot brown sandwich marries the flavors of ham and turkey with melted cheese, white bread, bacon and scallions. Or, if you prefer, try the salmon filet, blackened or grilled, with Hollandaise sauce. There's an award-winning spinach and artichoke dip to start your meal with. OVO is a non-smoking restaurant.

**Open: T–S 11 a.m.–2 p.m., 5:30–9 p.m., closed Su & M
MC V**

Did you know?
The oldest volunteer fire company in Indiana is the Fair Play Company No. 1, a fire station at Madison.

METAMORA

Restaurant nominated by Alberta Sauerland, clerk-treasurer, Brookville

Hearthstone Restaurant

**18149 US 52, Metamora, IN 47030
(765) 647-5204**

Located near quiet and beautiful, historic Metamora, one of the few canal era "boom towns," the Hearthstone is declared by Brookville Clerk-Treasurer Sauerland to have "one of the best homemade salad bars around." The pies and other desserts are also homemade specialties. Her favorite is the pan-fried chicken. The ham and catfish are said to be tasty, too. If surroundings look familiar, it's because scenes from the 1988 hit movie *Rainman* were shot here. Banquet facilities and catering are available. Reservations recom-mended on weekends.

**Open: 11 a.m.–9 p.m. T–Th, 10 a.m.–10 p.m. F–S,
10 a.m.–8 p.m. Su, closed M
MC V Di**

MILAN

Milan Railroad Inn

101 E. Carr St., Milan, IN 47031
(812) 654-2800 or 1-800-448-7405

If you have Hoosier hysteria, you'll delight in this old train depot full of memorabilia from the 1954 Milan High School State Basketball champions and Milan's own Jenny Johnson, the first "First Lady of Softball" inducted into the hall of fame, proudly displayed on the walls of the Railroad Inn. You'll find delicious Indiana fried chicken, steaks, chops, seafood, and a soup and salad bar to die for. Reservations accepted.

Open: 11 a.m.–8 p.m. Su–Th, 11 a.m.–9 p.m. F–S
MC V

Villa Milan Vineyard

7287 East CR 50 N, Milan, IN 47031
(812) 654-3419

Italian entrees at Villa Milan are complemented by estate bottled wine. After attending a free wine tasting, enjoy your meal on the gazebo where "the view is as intoxicating as the wines." With their unique European-style hard rolls, enjoy a glass of Villa Milan wine and the Italian chicken with pasta primavera. You must visit the Villa Milan Vineyard to experience this wine — it's sold only on-site. Reservations accepted.

Open: 9 a.m.–8 p.m. M–Th, 10 a.m.–9 p.m. F–S, closed Su
MC V Di

MILLHOUSEN

Restaurant nominated by Joe Johannigman, clerk-treasurer,
and L. June Ryle, clerk-treasurer, Greensburg.

Stone's

2356 E. High St., Millhousen, IN 47261
(812) 591-2435

Your tastebuds will thank you after trying the fried chicken at Stone's. The family atmosphere is made cozier by the warm fireplace in the red room. If you're not in the mood for chicken, try the grilled salmon or ribeye. A Wednesday buffet draws diners from all over. Reservations accepted for large parties.

Open: 5–9 p.m. W & F, 4–9:30 p.m. S
closed Su, M, T & Th
MC V

MITCHELL

Jack's Lounge & Restaurant

505 Main Street, Mitchell, IN 47446
(812) 849-9121

Lots of Hoosiers including the likes of IU Coach Bobby Knight have been known to frequent Jack's. It's rumored that the restaurant has the "largest prime rib known." Cash or check only. Sorry, no reservations.

Open: 11 a.m.–9 p.m. Su–Th, 11 a.m.–10 p.m. F–S

Did you know?
Two-thirds of Hoosiers live in a city or town.

OLDENBURG

Restaurant nominated by Mary Jo Dietz, clerk-treasurer

Brau Haus

Wasserstrasse, Oldenburg, IN 47036
(812) 934-4840

For an authentic taste of Germany, look for the church and convent towers looming above the hilltops of this German-settled "Town of Spires," and watch for the huge mural on the west wall of the Brau Haus, next to the parking lot. The fried chicken and salad bar are superb, according to Clerk-Treasurer Dietz, and well worth the drive. German beers, reasonable prices and a commitment to service are added enticements. Come and make yourself at home. Reservations accepted.

Open: 10 a.m.–9 p.m. M–Th, 10 a.m.–10 p.m. F–S,
11 a.m.–8 p.m. Su
MC V AmEx

Wagner's Village Inn

22171 Main St., Oldenburg, IN 47036
(812) 934-3854

Don't be fooled by the tavern-like facade: Wagner's is a large, family-oriented tavern/restaurant with friendly and fast service. Try to get in two meals in Oldenburg if only to savor the fried chicken at both Wagner's and Brau Haus, and then try to decide which is better. Local folks have been trying to decide for years. Steaks and seafood are also available. Reservations accepted.

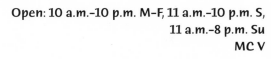

Open: 10 a.m.–10 p.m. M–F, 11 a.m.–10 p.m. S,
11 a.m.–8 p.m. Su
MC V

SEYMOUR

Restaurants nominated by John Burkhart, mayor.

Dakota Ridge

1400 Shields Ave., Seymour, IN 47274
(812) 524-0605

If you recognize the area around Dakota Ridge, it's because scenes from John Mellencamp's 1990 film *Falling From Grace* were shot here. Enjoy nine holes of golf at the former Seymour Country Club, then head for the sports bar where you can choose from over 100 domestic and imported beers. Or relax in the dining room and try Mayor Burkhart's favorite, Basil and Roasted Almond Crusted Salmon. His Honor also suggests the chef's signature Southwestern Dip as an appetizer. Weekend reservations accepted.

Open: 11 a.m.–11 p.m. T–Th, 11 a.m.–1 a.m. F–S,
closed Su & M
MC V AmEx Di

Larrison's Diner

200 S. Chestnut St., Seymour, IN 47274
(812) 522-5523

Multiple honors from appearing in the John Mellencamp film *Falling From Grace* to its own chapter in Bob Lilliefor's book *Hwy. 50: Ain't That America* have been bestowed upon Larrison's. The diner, famous for its old-style hamburgers and hand-dipped milkshakes, has been serving patrons for more than fifty years. Mayor Burkhart recommends a cheeseburger with fried onions, a side of fries, a cherry Pepsi and a chocolate shake. Cash or local checks only, please.

Open: 7 a.m.–3:45 p.m. M–Th & S,
7 a.m.–7:45 p.m. F, closed Su

Did you know?
Seymour is the only city in the United States to have a continuous annual observance for veterans since World War II, which has had a V-J Day parade each August since 1945.

The Townhouse Café

206 E. Fourth St., Seymour, IN 47274
(812) 522-1099

Local residents love The Townhouse Café so much that when financial problems in the early eighties threatened its closure, a group of twelve "regulars" each kicked in $500 and signed a loan to buy the place. They sold it in 1996 to its present owner, who waitressed there as a twelve-year-old. Part of its popularity is due to the biscuits and gravy and the $1.50 Giant Cinnamon Roll. Cash or check only please.

Open: 5 a.m.–2 p.m. M & S, 5 a.m.–8 p.m. T–F, 7 a.m.–2 p.m. Su

Gerth Café

119 E. Second St., Seymour, IN 47274
(812) 522-3860

Open 365 days a year, the Gerth Café has been a local favorite for over 60 years. Mayor Burkhart recommends the tenderloin, white beans and fried potatoes. Sorry, no reservations and no credit cards.

Open: 4 a.m.–10 p.m. M–S
4–11 a.m. & 2 (usually!)–10 p.m. Su

VINCENNES

Restaurants nominated by Howard W. Hatcher, mayor.

Charlie's Smorgasboard

630 Kimmell Road, Vincennes, IN 47591
(812) 882-5115

Folks from all over have been coming to Charlie's for almost a half-century. Mayor Hatcher says the Sunday-style cooking every day of the week draws diners from near and far. His Honor favors the chicken and dumplings. Other popular entrées include fried chicken, pork chops, liver, fish and baked chicken. Reservations available for large parties.

Open: 10:30 a.m.–8 p.m. M–Th, 10:30 a.m.–9 p.m. F–S

Old Thyme Diner

331 Main St., Vincennes, IN 47591
(812) 886-0333

Step back in time to the turn of the last century at the Old Thyme Diner, where the beef Manhattans are spectacular and the grilled tenderloin and fries can't be beat. Mayor Hatcher says you'd better get there early, though, because people come from all over and the tables fill up fast! Cash only.

Open: 8 a.m.–2 p.m. M–Th & S, 8 a.m–8 p.m. F

Did you know?
From 1800 to 1813, Vincennes served as the Indiana Territory capital under Governor William Henry Harrison.

Pea-Fections

323 Main St., Vincennes, IN 47591
(812) 886-5146

A relaxing atmosphere coupled with quick and courteous service makes Pea-Fections a popular lunch spot with local businessmen. Try soup and a sandwich, or one of the daily specials. Be sure to save room for their famous desserts! (The Strawberry Creme Torte is the employee favorite.) Reservations available for parties of six or more.

Open: 11 a.m.–2 p.m., m–F, 11 a.m.–3 p.m. S, closed Su
MC V AmEx Di

WASHINGTON

Restaurants nominated by Tom Baumert, mayor

The Black Buggy

910 Hwy 57 S, Washington, IN 47501
(812) 254-8966

If an Amish buffet sounds good, head to The Black Buggy. You'll find a wide selection of food on the buffet, including three kinds of meat. Specialties are prime rib Mondays and seafood on Fridays. Mayor Baumert says to get there early or be ready to stand in line. Carry-out and drive-through service available. Reservations available weekdays.

Open: 6 a.m.–9 p.m. M–Su, closed Su
MC V AmEx Di

Did you know?
The largest expense for most municipalities over 5,000 people is police and fire protection. The next most-expensive items are streets and parks.

Hunan Garden

207 E. National Rd., Washington, IN 47501
(812) 254-7568

Authentic Chinese food will sizzle your tastebuds while you treat the rest of your senses to the sights and music of China at Hunan Garden. Mayor Baumert recommends the sour chicken and pork.

Open: 11 a.m.–8:30 p.m. T–Su, closed M
MC V AmEx Di

The New White Steamer

21 E. Main St., Washington, IN 47501
(812) 254-9973

Mayor Baumert says once you get a whiff of the cooked onions wafting down Main Street, you won't be able to resist stopping by The New White Steamer. He recommends the burgers and chili. Cash only, please.

Open: 5 a.m.–6 p.m. M–Th, 5 a.m.–7 p.m. F,
5 a.m.–4 p.m. S, closed Su

SOUTHERN

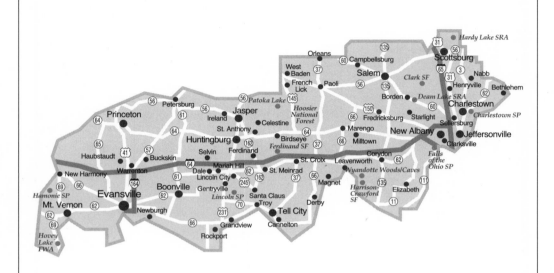

The southlands are graced by two great rivers, majestic hills, the site of Abraham Lincoln's youth – and Hoosier fried chicken!

Two great rivers and a thousand rolling hills grace the glacier-formed landscape of the historic and scenic Southland of Indiana.

Once, the Wabash and Ohio Rivers were the major avenues for travelers and commerce, Today they are complemented by two great Interstate Highways: the east-west I-64 and the north-south I-65. These expansive roadways are joined by other national and improved state highway tributaries to provide pleasant passage throughout this land of historic enchantment and extraordinary Hometown dining opportunities.

Here you'll find the boyhood home of Abraham Lincoln, Indiana's first State Capitol, Devonian Age fossil beds and riverboat casinos— modern-day versions of the paddle-wheeled ships which plied their trade up and down the beautiful Ohio River which creates Indiana's shared southern border with Kentucky.

You also will discover the urban wonders of great cities such as Evansville, New Albany and Jeffersonville, treasure-filled museums, historic mansions and other opportunities for adventure and personal enrichment.

Along the southern Wabash River that serves as the western boundary of the Southern Tourism Region is the state's best-preserved early Indiana community—New Harmony. The site of two communal living experiments in the early nineteenth century, this peaceful town is well worth an extended visit, especially if you select lodgings at the New Harmony Inn, a uniquely designed forty-five-room facility which captures the spirit of the community's past. There are no radios or television sets, but you will be thrilled by the quality of the architecture, the art-filled public areas and poplar plank flooring. We suggest you ask for a room with a fireplace and northern view of the pond that lies behind this charming inn. Plan at least a full day to fully appreciate the living legacy of George Rapp's followers who first settled there in 1814, followed by the utopian experiment of Welsh industrialist Robert Owen and Scottish philanthropist Robert Maclure. Some of the world's most famous scientists and teachers arrived there on the "Boatload of Knowledge" in 1826 to test their theory that the key to a better life was education. Discover which of the two experiments succeeded: The Rappites, based on hard labor and celibacy or the Owenites, based on education and cultural pursuits? Begin your quest at the New Harmony Visitor Center in the Atheneum at North and Arthur streets. Following a film, which depicts the history of the community, visit the exhibits at the center. Guided walking tours are recommended although maps for self-guided excursions are available. Among today's more popular stops on the tour is the Labyrinth, a reconstruction of the one designed by the original Harmonist settlers at Historic New Harmony's visitor center. The winding maze of the labyrinth is meant to symbolize the difficult path one must follow to achieve true harmony. The centerpiece of a brick-walled courtyard designed by world-famous architect Philip Johnson is The Roofless Church which houses a sculpture of The Madonna created by artist Jacques Lipchitz. For details call (812) 682-4488. Artistry of a different sort is created each day at New Harmony's Red Geranium Inn where the Shaker Lemon Pie and Chocolate Vinegar Cake are local sweet treat favorites.

After a memorable dinner of bratwurst and sauerkraut at Gundi's in Mount Vernon in the southwest "pocket corner" of Indiana, your tour should meander upriver to the vibrant riverfront community of Evansville. This city is undergoing a dazzling regeneration along its riverfront and elsewhere. Sparked to a degree by new revenue from the riverfront Casino Aztar, the city has set about to develop its downtown and restore its historic structures such as the old Victory Theatre and the old United States Post Office, Court House and Custom House. Others benefiting from the restoration renaissance include The Pagoda. Built in 1913 as a shelter house and bandstand, the structure has undergone a $2 million refurbishing and now is the home of the Evansville Convention and Visitors Bureau—a good place to begin your exploration of Evansville. A popular favorite at The Pagoda visitor center is the Riverfront Walking Tour Guide featuring all thirty-nine riverfront historic homes and attractions. Some of our favorite walking tour stops include the Evansville Museum of Arts and Science, 411 E. Riverside Drive, and the John Augustus Reitz Home Museum, 224 S. First Street. Built in 1871, the French Second Empire Reitz home has elaborate architectural features and contains many original pieces of furniture. Call

(812) 426-1871 or visit their web site, www.reitzhome.evansville.net for details. Great gifts for the sweet of tooth are available at the locally owned and operated Lib's Candies Stores. There's one at 601 E. Main Street which we favor because of their friendly sales staff. Other Main Street Walkway visits we'd suggest are The Jungle Restaurant, Bar & Cigar Lounge, 415 Main Street, a renovated 1875-built facility which won an Indiana Main Street Restoration Award. The bar and lounge are located in the basement level with the restaurant and coffeehouse on the street level. We also like to browse for bargains at deJong's Clothing Store, 306 Main Street. For the latest news and information about Downtown Evansville visit their lively web site: www.downtownevansville.org.

Now head east where renovation continues on some pre-historic structures. About five hundred years prior to the construction of the Reitz Home, Native Americans of the Middle Mississippian culture were constructing abodes and tall mounds at the nearby 103-acre Angel Mounds State Historic Site, 8215 Pollack Ave. The largest of eleven major mounds covers four acres and is forty-four feet in height. An interpretive center houses exhibits of Native American culture and artifacts unearthed at the site of the fourteenth- and fifteenth-century city, where about one thousand persons are believed to have lived. Open year round, details are available by calling (812) 853-3956.

No trip to the Evansville area is complete without a stop at Indiana's Number One Favorite Hometown Restaurant, The Log Inn, twelve miles north via U.S. 41, where the family style chicken dinners are an historical event. Abe Lincoln himself once dined in this oldest and best restaurant in Indiana.

About two miles east of Angel Mounds is the charming riverfront town of Newburgh, the only Indiana town captured and looted during the Civil War by someone other than Confederate cavalry legend John Hunt Morgan. The capture of the town is one of the more fascinating stories of Indiana's role in the Civil War. However, your first stop will be at the offices of Historic Newburgh Inc., 9 W. Jennings Street, (State Road 662) to pick up a map for your self-guided walking tour [phone: (812) 853-2815]. Your next stop will be at 1 Jennings Street, the old Exchange Hotel built in 1841. In 1862 the hotel was being used as a hospital and was filled with wounded Union soldiers. It was looted of food and medical items by the bold Confederate guerilla Adam R. (Stovepipe) Johnson. The story goes that with a handful of soldiers and a rowboat Johnson approached the town via the Ohio River from Kentucky and duped the town defenders into believing that several stovepipes he had placed atop logs on a hill on the Kentucky side of the river were powerful cannons. As the town leaders peered on the opposite shore at what appeared to be the formidable weapons, they surrendered and the pillaging began. Now it's your turn to pillage the charming specialty stores and gift shops that are sprinkled between historic homes, fine restaurants and art galleries in historic Newburgh.

From Newburgh we suggest a trip to Lincoln City and the Lincoln Boyhood National Memorial. It was at this farm that Lincoln spent fourteen of the most formative years of his life. Attractions include The Memorial Visitor Center honoring Abraham Lincoln and the burial place of the president's mother, Nancy Hanks Lincoln. Exhibits focus on the lives of the Lincolns as pioneers in the Indiana wilderness. Your tour should begin by viewing a 24-minute film entitled, "Here I Grew Up." Call (812) 937-4541 or visit the web site, www.nps.gov/libo, for additional information.

Today's youth will delight at the Town of Santa Claus just east of the Lincoln Memorial. After a visit to Santa's post office, we suggest the rest of the day be spent at Holiday World and Splashin' Safari, where the Raven roller coaster will provide an ocean of thrills. The ride was recently named among America's Top Ten roller coasters by Forbes *American Heritage* magazine. The complex includes Indiana's largest interactive waterplay and slide facility. Call ahead, (800) 927-2571, or visit their web site, www.holidayworld.com.

A more tranquil ride north to Jasper is our next recommendation. Take State Road 162 through the scenic community of Ferdinand and, if it's mealtime, Ferdy's Flyer is our Hometown Restaurant pick for lunch or a snack. The castle-like structure on the large hill overlooking Ferdinand is the Monastery of the Immaculate Conception. Operated by the Benedictine Order of Women, guided tours and a gift shop, "For Heaven's Sake," are among the attractions. Next, for the sake of your appetite, we strongly recommend you schedule time up the road at Jasper for a Germanic feast at The Schnitzelbank, a Hometown Top Ten Restaurant. Look for the Glockenspiel Tower and the new Hampton Inn Motel next to this extraordinary family-owned and operated dining establishment. Visitor attractions at Jasper include the Indiana Baseball Hall of Fame at State Road 231 and College Avenue. Architectural fans also will want to visit the Holy Family Church just off highway 162 on Jasper's southeast side which features the nation's second largest stained-glass window. At 13th and Newton streets is St. Joseph Church, an 1880 Romanesque structure listed on the National Register of Historic Places. For details on these and other area visitor attractions visit or contact the Dubois County Tourism Commission, 610 Main Street, (800) 968-4578. The web site is www.duboiscounty.org.

From Jasper we suggest you drop down to Interstate 64 and motor east to Leavenworth. Even if you're not hungry, stop at the Overlook Restaurant for the panoramic view of the Ohio River from the deck behind this Top Ten Favorite Hometown treasure.

Within easy driving distance from Leavenworth is the state's first Capitol, Corydon, where you'll find unique crafts and other specialty shops at the Emporium Mall, on the town's historic square. The mall is directly across the street from the Corydon Capitol State Historic Site, an 1816 limestone structure at 202 E. Walnut Street

If you favor underground adventure, near Corydon is Squire Boone Caverns, discovered in 1790 by Daniel Boone and his brother, Squire Boone, who is buried there. Attractions at Boone's Caverns include tours, gemstone mining and the largest rock shop in the Midwest. The working gristmill originally built by Squire Boone, features an eighteen-foot wheel powered by waters flowing from the caverns. Exhibits inside the mill include original foundation stones from the mill on which Boone had inscribed, "My God my life hath much befriended. I'll praise Him till my days are ended." More information is available via the caverns' web site, www.squireboonecaverns.com. Also near Corydon is Marengo Cave, a National Landmark, consistently ranked as one of America's ten most beautiful show caves. Discovered in 1883, the 122-acre facility offers cave tours, campgrounds, a swimming pool, horseback riding and canoe and kayak rentals. We suggest a visit to their informative web site, www.cavern.com/marengocave.

Another unique attraction nearby is the Needmore Buffalo Farm at Elizabeth. There, tours of the five-hundred-acre farm where 140 buffalo roam are among several entertainment options available. Drop in on their web site for details, www.nmbfarm.com.

Upriver from Elizabeth, about fifteen miles via scenic State Road 111, is the Falls of the Ohio Interpretive Center, located at the site of the world's largest exposed Devonian-age fossil bed, including a 386-million-year-old fossilized coral reef. A film and exhibits enlighten visitors to this 220-acre relic of the distant past. Web site for the center is www.fallsoftheohio.org.

Among the other numerous visitor attractions in the historic metropolitan Clarksville-Jeffersonville-New Albany area, directly across the Ohio River from Louisville, Kentucky, some are worth special mention. The Carnegie Center for Art and History, 201 E. Spring Street, and the Culbertson Mansion State Historic Site, 914 E. Main Street, both in New Albany, are in that special category. The twenty-five-room Victorian Culbertson mansion features a rosewood staircase and crystal chandeliers reflecting the affluence of its builder, William S. Culbertson, who once was considered the wealthiest person in Indiana. Wealth is the goal of visitors to the world's largest gaming vessel, *The Glory of Rome*, a floating Caesars Indiana Casino, downriver in nearby Bridgeport. Firefighting buffs will want to race to the new Conway Fire Museum, 402 Mount Tabor Rd., New Albany, featuring vintage hand-, horse-, and steam-powered fire equipment. You may also visit via the museum's web site, www.conwayfiremuseum.org. Steam power also propelled this area to great wealth in bygone days and the story is told in a converted mansion which now houses the Howard Steamboat Museum, 1101 E. Market Street, Jeffersonville. No visit to Jeffersonville is complete without a stop at the state's oldest candy store, Schimpff's Confectionery. The 108-year-old facility offers lunch at an old fashioned soda fountain where diners can view the original tin ceiling. Serious diners, however, should plan an evening at The Inn On Spring, a block away, where elegant continental cuisine will provide a mouth-watering crown to your visit to the "Sunnyside" of the Ohio River.

For details on this and other Clarksville-New Albany-Jeffersonville area attractions visit the visitor's bureau web site, www.sunnysideoflouisville.org.

And, finally, we know of no better way to end your tour of scenic Southern Indiana than a trip to the beautiful Knobs area northwest of New Albany and a visit to Joe Huber's Family Farm, Orchard, and Restaurant. Located near the community of Starlight, the 250-acre Huber facility is in one of the most productive fruit and vegetable regions in the Midwest. For details on special events at the farm, we suggest you visit the family web site, www.joehubers.com or call ahead, (812) 923-5255. It's Hoosier family fun at its satisfying best. Owned and operated for four generations of the Huber family, attractions include a large farm market and gift shop, tractor wagon tours, a winery and live entertainment. The Huber Family Restaurant, given a four-star rating by the *Louisville Courier-Journal*, offers an extensive menu, but a local favorite is the fried chicken with biscuits and apple butter, topped off with a juicy slab of homemade peach cobbler.

Indiana's Favorite Hometown Restaurants

From New Harmony to Starlight, we're sure you'll find the extraordinary dining opportunities and illuminating visitor attractions in this Southern Wonderland to be the perfect recipe for sweet memories.

For more information, contact the following visitors centers:

Clark-Floyd Counties .... (812) 288-2634
Evansville .... (800) 433-3025
Harrison County .... (812) 738-2137
Perry County .... (888) 343-6262
Scott County .... (812) 752-7270
Washington County .... (812) 883-4303
Dubois County .... (800) 968-4578
Crawford County .... (888) 846-5397
Spencer County .... (888) 444-9252

Did you know?
The first civil settlement in the Northwest Territory in what became Indiana was Clarksville. It became the state's first incorporated town. The town book was begun in 1784.

CLARKSVILLE

Sun Set Grill

318 W. Highway 131, Clarksville, IN 47129
(812) 945-3496

Surround yourself in the past at the Sun Set Grill, a restored historic home built around 1870. You'll enjoy the beautiful interior almost as much as the executive chef's beef, chicken and seafood creations. Ask about his special "sunburnt" Cajun seasoning. The coconut shrimp is the house specialty, but be sure to try the chicken marsala with mushroom sauce or the chicken Anthony topped with red wine marinara. Reservations accepted.

Open: 11 a.m.–9 p.m. M–Th, 11a.m.–10 p.m. F–S, 11 a.m.–8 p.m. Su
MC V AmEx

DALE

Windell's Café

Hwy. 62 East, Dale, IN 47523
(812) 937-4253

Since 1947 diners have enjoyed the fare at Windell's Café, where they can sit at the horseshoe shaped bar and enjoy a "cup o' joe." Dubbed "The Eating Place of Mid-America's Crossroads," Windell's will tempt your tastebuds with their homemade chicken and dumplings or ribs and sauerkraut. And top it all off with a piece of mouth-watering homemade pie for dessert. This is a nonalcoholic, family establishment. Reservations accepted for large parties. Cash only.

Open: 5 a.m.–8 p.m. daily

EVANSVILLE

Turoni's Pizzery & Brewery

TWO LOCATIONS: 4 N. Weinbach Ave., Evansville, IN 47715
(812) 477-7500
AND 408 N. Main St., Evansville, IN 47713
(812) 424-9871

Former residents regularly return to Evansville just to satisfy their cravings for undoubtedly the best pizza in Indiana at Turoni's. For more than 30 years, they've been serving up extra-special pizza. Choose from four cheese toppings; vegetables including fresh spinach, artichoke hearts and fresh chopped garlic; and meats including country bacon, grilled chicken and even low-fat ground emu. There's also a selection of gourmet pizzas including Hawaiian Delite, Cheesy-Cheese, Buffalo-Style Chicken, and Vincenzio's Masterpiece-A. If you can't make up your mind, try the House Special. Call-ahead seating available. Reservations accepted Su–Th.

Open: 11 a.m.–11 p.m. M–Th, 11 a.m.–midnight F, noon–midnight S, 4–11 p.m. Su
MC V Di

Did you know?
At 67 acres, Mesker Park Zoo in Evansville is the state's largest zoo.

FERDINAND

Restaurant nominated by Charles Schuler, councilmember

Ferdy Flyer

133 W. 10th St., Ferdinand, IN 47523
(812) 367-2222

Time flies for train and food lovers at the Ferdy Flyer, with a hearty serving of Hoosier hospitality, according to Councilmember Schuler. While dining on turtle soup, fried chicken or burgers, you can enjoy looking at the restaurant's collection of historic memorabilia from the Ferdy Flyer Railroad which served Ferdinand some years ago. Just five miles long, it was the shortest railroad in the state. A sign on the roof of the restaurant is a replica of the Ferdy Flyer train. Reservations advised.

Open: 8 a.m.–9 p.m. M–Th, 8 a.m.–10 p.m. F–Su
MC V Di DC

HAUBSTADT

Restaurants nominated by Bonnie Wagner, clerk-treasurer

Haub House

105 Main St., Haubstadt, IN 47639
(812) 768-6462

The locals know that about the only thing to pass by Haub's are the trains that rumble through town along the tracks out front. Inside, you'll find some of the most tender prime rib you'll ever taste. Order fried mushrooms for an appetizer and a twice-baked potato on the side for a memorable meal. The seafood is good, too. There's an early bird menu for diners between 4–6 p.m. Reservations recommended.

Open: 4 p.m.–10 p.m. M–S, closed Su
MC V AmEx Di

Carriage Inn

103 E. Gibson St., Haubstadt, IN 47639
(812) 768-6131

The daily lunch specials are what keep Clerk-Treasurer Wagner coming back to the Carriage Inn. Tasty sandwiches and a relaxing atmosphere make it a great place to unwind

from a hectic day. Evening specials and family-style dining for large parties round out the menu. Reservations accepted.

Open: 10:30 a.m.–10 p.m. M–S, closed Su
MC V AmEx Di

IRELAND

The Chicken Place

Hwy 56, Ireland, IN 47545
(812) 482-7600

For some out-of-this-world fried chicken, be sure to visit the Chicken Place. Regulars rave about the delicious German fries, too. Located in the heart of Ireland, once you're in town, you can't miss it! And the restaurant boasts a new, expanded parking area. Jasper Mayor Bill Schmitt and Little Jimmy Dickens brag about The Chicken Place. Reservations are accepted M–Th only.

Open: 4:30–9 p.m. M–F, 3:30–9 p.m. S, closed Su & holidays
MC V

Did you know?
The first city in the nation to discontinue garbage collection and install waste disposers in each house was Jasper, on August 1, 1950. The reduction in taxes was expected to help pay for the costs of the disposers.

JASPER

Restaurant nominated by Nancy Eckerle, councilmember

Yaggi's Restaurant

514 Jackson St., Jasper, IN 47546
(812) 482-4200

If you're looking for a comfortable place to relax with friends, head to Yaggi's. The homey atmosphere, good service and low prices make it a hit with Councilmember Eckerle. She recommends the barbecued smoked pork chop or breaded tenderloin. Nightly specials round out the menu. Reservations accepted for parties of eight or more.

Open: 5:30 a.m.–9 p.m. M-F, 5:30 a.m.–10 p.m. S,
3–9 p.m. Su (bar only)
MC V Di

JEFFERSONVILLE

Restaurant nominated by Bill Schmitt, mayor, Jasper

Big Daddy's Bar-Be-Que

108 Eastern Blvd., Jeffersonville, IN 47130
(812) 284-9790

For the finest pulled pork and tenderest pork ribs around, head straight for Big Daddy's. Their hickory-smoked meats defy description. You won't be sorry.

Open: 11 a.m.–8 p.m. M-Th, 11 a.m.–9 p.m. F-S, closed Su
MC V AmEx

Restaurants nominated by Thomas Galligan, mayor

Buckhead Mountain Grill

707 W. Riverside Dr., Jeffersonville, IN 47130
(812) 284-2919

Located on the Jeffersonville riverfront between the bridges, the Buckhead Mountain Grill serves up great food with mile-high friendliness. The view is spectacular and the atmosphere will remind you of an Aspen ski lodge. Mayor Galligan recommends the ribs, steak and chicken pot pie. Sorry, no reservations.

Open: 11 a.m.–10:30 p.m. M-Th, 11 a.m.–11:30 p.mF-S,
11 a.m.–9:30 p.m. Su
MC V AmEx Di

Did you know?
The nation's largest inland shipyard is Jeffboat, Inc., located at Jeffersonville. The company has launched over 6,200 vessels since it was founded in 1938.

The Inn on Spring

415 Spring St., Jeffersonville, IN 47130
(812) 284-5545

Fine dining is alive and well in historic downtown Jeffersonville. Reminiscent of a European café, The Inn on Spring is your gateway to an unforgettable dining experience. The elegant continental cuisine changes seasonally. Try the roast leg of lamb, or the seafood tostada filled with fish, shrimp, scallops and lobster with cheese and vegetables. Reservations advised.

Open: 11:30 a.m.–1 p.m. T–F, 6–9 p.m. W–S, closed Su
MC V AmEx

Rocky's Sub Pub

1207 E. Market St., Jeffersonville, IN 47130
(812) 282-3844

You won't find better pizza than at Rocky's, voted Best Restaurant in Southern Indiana by readers of *Louisville* magazine. Their secret is in the homemade crust. Try a whole wheat or regular crust and pile on the fresh toppings. The subs and salads are popular, too. Reservations recommended on weekends.

Open: 11 a.m.–10 p.m. T–Th, 11 a.m.–11 p.m. F, 4–11 p.m. S, 4–10 p.m. Su, closed M
MC V AmEx

Schimpff's Confectionary

347 Spring St., Jeffersonville, IN 47130
(812) 283-8367

Producing hand-made candies since 1891, Schimpff's has been family operated for four generations. Located in a Civil War-era building that features the original tin ceiling and a 1950s soda fountain, Schimpff's will delight your tastebuds with lunch specials and sweet treats to savor after your meal. Try some of the famous red hots (watch out—they're really hot!), fish candy and Modjeskas. For lunch, Mayor Galligan recommends the chicken salad sandwich and potato salad. Sorry, no reservations.

Open: 10 a.m.–5 p.m. M–F, 10 a.m.–3 p.m. S, closed Su
MC V

CANNELTON

Restaurant nominated by Bill Goffinet, mayor, Tell City

Patio Steak House

Highway 66 W, Cannelton, IN 47520
(812) 547-4949

The outstanding salad bar at the Patio is a Southern Indiana favorite. While you're trying to decide between the selection of steaks, seafood and pasta, take a look at the unique paddle fan in the dining area. If you can't make up your mind, Mayor Goffinet suggests the New York strip steak. Prices range from $6 to $20. Reservations accepted for large parties only.

Open: 11 a.m.–9:30 p.m. M–Th, 11 a.m.–10:30 p.m. F–S,
11 a.m.–3 p.m. Su
MC V AmEx Di

MILLTOWN

Restaurant nominated by Lula M. Combs, clerk-treasurer,
and William Dubois, councilmember

Blue River Café

128 West Main St., Milltown, IN 47145
(812) 633-7510

Housed in the oldest building in a small town once famous for its mill and limestone kilns, the Blue River Café has the unanimous endorsement of Milltown's elected leaders, who favor the café's relaxing atmosphere. They recommend the white chili, orange roughy and vegetarian entrees. Reservations advised.

Open: 11 a.m.–9 p.m. F–S, 11 a.m.–3 p.m. Su, closed M–Th
MC V

MOUNT VERNON

Gundi's Restaurant

132 E. Second St. (at the corner of 2nd & Walnut),
Mt. Vernon, IN 47620
(812) 838-4661

Get a taste of Southern Indiana's German heritage at Gundi's, where you'll find delicious German and American foods. A highly recommended meal is the bratwurst, sauerkraut, mashed potatoes and Northern beans. And leave room for dessert. More than one diner has claimed they have the best pies in Southern Indiana. Reservations available.

Open: T–S 5:30 a.m.–8 p.m., 5:30 a.m.–3 p.m. Su, M closed
MC V AmEx Di

New Albany

Kelsey's Bar & Grill

730 Rolling Creek Dr., New Albany, IN 47150
(812) 949-1001

Outstanding service and a friendly atmosphere make Kelsey's a favorite among the locals. The award-winning hot wings with both the chef's special sauce and the con queso sauce come highly recommended. Reservations accepted.

**Open: 11 a.m.–midnight M–F, noon–midnight S, closed Su
MC V AmEx Di**

New Harmony

The Red Geranium Restaurant

504 North St., New Harmony, IN 47631
(812) 682-4431

Stay overnight in the historic New Harmony Inn, and stroll down the street to The Red Geranium Restaurant. For over 30 years, The Red Geranium has provided great food and service in a cozy country inn atmosphere. Local officials recommend tempting your tastebuds with the Char prime steak, spinach salad and Shaker lemon pie. Reservations advised. For more, check out www.redg.com.

**Open: 11 a.m.–10 p.m. T–S, 11 a.m.–8 p.m. Su, closed M
MC V AmEx Di**

Did you know?
The town of New Harmony is home to the first public school system.

Newburgh

Restaurants nominated by Jack Chaddock, councilmember

Edgewater Grill

1 E. Water St., Newburgh, IN 47630
(812) 858-2443

Enjoy a beautiful sunset on the Ohio River from an outdoor table on one of the decks at Edgewater Grill. An extensive wine list complements any entrée. Select from the catch of the day or meal of the day, or sample something delicious from the menu. The pizza, cooked in a brick oven, is a winner with Councilman Chaddock. Reservations accepted for parties of 10 or more.

Open: 10 a.m.–10 p.m. M–Th, 11 a.m.–11 p.m. F–S, closed Su
MC V AmEx Di

Knob Hill Tavern

1016 Highway 662 W, Newburgh, IN 47630
(812) 853-9550

For years, locals have gathered at Knob Hill which features casual dining at its best. Dine in the cozy tavern or treat the family in the family room. Councilman Chaddock recommends the catfish fiddlers. You'll know you are in the right spot when you see the distinctive flashing catfish neon sign. Reservations accepted weekdays.

Open: 11 a.m.–10 p.m. M–Th, 11 a.m.–11 p.m. F–S, noon–9 p.m. Su
MC V AmEx Di

The Old Homestead Inn

10233 State Road 662, Newburgh, IN 47630
(812) 853-3631

The "Homestead" is an institution in southwestern Indiana, where generations of area families love to gather for delicious fine food served in a country atmosphere. Those who know say the fried chicken is among the best that you'll find anywhere. Try the corn fritters and honey butter, too. Reservations accepted.

Open: 5–8 p.m. W–S, 11 a.m.–2 p.m. Su, closed M–T
MC V Di

SCOTTSBURG

Jeeves & Company

64 S. Main St., Scottsburg, IN 47170
(812) 752-6559

Located in a turn-of-the-century building on the West side of the Courthouse square, Jeeves & Company is a true find. Gourmet entrées include Steak with Mustard Cream Dressing, Bourbon Pecan Chicken and Creole Chicken Alfredo. For a lighter meal, try the Portobello Mushroom, marinated in Balsamic vinegar and served with Bordelaise sauce, and a Chicken Spinach Salad topped with hot poppy seed dressing. Reservations recommended.

Open: 9 a.m.–5 p.m. M, 9 a.m.–8 p.m. T–Th,
9 a.m.–9 p.m. F–S, 11 a.m.–3 p.m. Su
MC V AmEx Di

Mariann Restaurant

Hwy 56 East, just off I-65, Scottsburg, IN 47170
(812) 752-5666

People come from all around to grab a stack of Mariann's Famous Hotcakes. Made from a secret Pirtle Family Recipe, the pancakes are so famous that the mix is now available to buy and, in fact, is shipped all over the country. Purists will love the traditional pancakes. For the more adventuresome, try the chocolate chip, blueberry, blackberry or raspberry variety. Breakfast is served any time. The rest of the menu sounds pretty good, too. Sorry, no reservations.

Open: 6 a.m.–9 p.m. daily
MC V AmEx

SELLERSBURG

Restaurant nominated by Gary Fenner, councilmember

Skip Jack's Fish on the Fly

490 N. Indiana Ave., Sellersburg, IN 47172
(812) 246-6346

"This is not your normal fish place," proclaims Councilmember Fenner. The unique flavor of the breading on the fish and the massive amounts of food on your plate make Skip Jack's a hit. Try the fish and onion rings, and treat yourself to any of the homemade side dishes and pies. Cash only.

Open: 11 a.m.–8 p.m. M–Th, 11 a.m.–9 p.m. F–S, closed Su

STARLIGHT

Joe Huber Family Farm, Orchard & Restaurant

2421 Scottsville Rd., Starlight, IN 47106
(812) 923-5255

Meander down winding roads as you leave the fast lane behind you on your way to Joe Huber's, where seven generations of the Huber family have nurtured the soil. When you arrive, you'll find country cooking just like Grandma's served family-style. Specials include country-fried chicken, Huber honey ham, fried biscuits with apple butter, homestyle vegetables (locally grown!), chicken and dumplings and homemade fruit cobblers. Reservations recommended.

Open: 11 a.m.–8 p.m. M–Th, 11 a.m.–9 p.m. F–S, 11 a.m.–6 p.m. Su
MC V

TELL CITY

Restaurant nominated by Bill Goffinet, mayor

Capers Restaurant

701 Main St., Tell City, IN 47586
(812) 547-3333

Add Southern Indiana hospitality and area history together and you get Capers. The restaurant is located in a building listed on the National Register of Historic Places and features much of the original interior and exterior. Among the more unusual menu offerings is the white chili. You also can find steaks, pasta, pizza, seafood and sandwiches, all priced between $4 and $20. Reservations accepted for parties of eight or more.

Open: 4–10:30 p.m. Su–M, 11 a.m.–10:30 p.m. T–Th,
11 a.m.–midnight F–S
MC V AmEx Di

TENNYSON

Restaurants nominated by Kenneth Helming, clerk-treasurer

B & R Family Inn

110 S. Main St., Tennyson, IN 47637
(812) 567-8893

If the breakfast and lunch specials don't make you feel relaxed at the B & R Family Inn, the weekend entertainment will.

Clerk-Treasurer Helming is partial to the fiddler dinners here, but also recommends the fried chicken without hesitation. Cash only. Sorry, no reservations.

Open: 6 a.m.–8 p.m. M–Th, 6 a.m.–8:30 p.m. F–S,
noon–midnight Su (bar only)

Carolyn's Country Pizzeria

6788 N. State Road 161, Tennyson, IN 47537
(812) 567-4444

If you're looking for just plain good pizza in a relaxed, alcohol-free atmosphere, head for Carolyn's. Clerk-Treasurer Helming recommends the stromboli and any of the homemade desserts. Fried chicken and hamburgers are local favorites. The all glass dining room offers a great view of the "tree house" which was recently added. Cash or check only.

Open: 3–9 p.m. T–Th, 3–10 p.m. F–S, closed Su–M

The Country Rose Café

200 S. Main St., Tennyson, IN 47637
(812) 567-7673

You may be a stranger when you walk in, but when you leave you'll be like one of the family at the Country Rose Café. The country kitchen atmosphere featuring roses and hummingbirds will make you feel right at home. Choose from one of the 38 sandwiches on the menu, or try the liver and onions. Clerk-Treasurer Helming says their French toast is the best in southern Indiana. Cash or check only. Reservations recommended.

Open: 4 a.m.–1:30 p.m. M–F, 5–7 p.m. M–W & F,
5 p.m.–8:30 p.m. S, 6 a.m.–2 p.m. Su

WESTERN

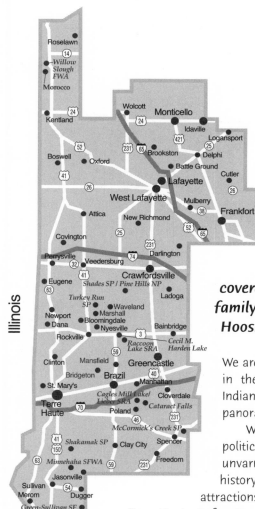

Roselawn
(14)
Willow
Slough
FWA
Morocco
Kentland
(24)
Boswell
(52)
Oxford
(41)
(26)
Attica
Covington
Perrysville
(32) Veedersburg
Eugene
(63) (41)
Newport
Dana
Rockville
Clinton Mansfield
Bridgeton
St. Mary's
Terre
Haute (70)
Shakamak SP
(41)
(150)
(63) Minnehaha SFWA
Sullivan
Merom
Green-Sullivan SF
Carlisle (58) Pleasantville
Jasonville
(54)
Dugger

Wolcott
(24) Monticello
Idaville
(421) Logansport
(231) (65) Brookston (25)
Delphi
Battle Ground
Cutler
Lafayette
(26)
West Lafayette
Mulberry
New Richmond (38) Frankfort
(25) (52)
(231) (65)
(231) Darlington
(74)
Crawfordsville
Shades SP / Pine Hills NP
Ladoga
Turkey Run
SP Waveland
Marshall
Bloomingdale
Nyesville
Bainbridge
(3)
Raccoon Cecil M.
Lake SRA Harden Lake
(59)
Greencastle
Brazil (40)
Manhattan
Cagles Mill Lake/
Lieber SRA Cloverdale
Poland Cataract Falls
(46) (231)
McCormick's Creek SP
Clay City Spencer
(59) Freedom
(231)

Illinois

Historic battles, colorful covered bridges and Indiana Beach family outings lure visitors to Hoosierland's western region

We are sure your touring and dining experiences in the scenic and historic Western region of Indiana will fill your days and evenings with a panorama of pleasure.

With its rich history, as well as its ethnic and political heritage, the Western region offers an unvarnished view of pioneer life, pre-statehood history and a colorful array of cosmopolitan attractions in its larger cities. Urban areas such as Terre Haute, Lafayette and West Lafayette where Purdue University has been producing astronauts and engineers since 1869 are a pleasant contrast to the rustic charm of smaller communities which house hidden treasures of dining and cultural delight.

Renown authors, statesmen, poets and world-changing ideas have sprung from this scenic shoulder of the Hoosier State.

A good jumping off point is Terre Haute, the economic and cultural Capital of West Central Indiana. After a visit to Indiana Pacer Coach and National Basketball Association legend Larry Bird's restaurant/hotel at 555 S. Third Street, and the Vigo County Historical Museum to see the first Coca Cola bottle that was designed in Terre Haute, we suggest a short visit to nearby Brazil. We also recommend you choose the less-traveled Old National Road route via U.S. 40. Located about fifteen miles east of Terre Haute is Brazil's most popular and patriotic restaurant, the Blue Bonnet. There, amidst the red-white-and-blue décor, you may find Mayor Ken Crabb enjoying barbecued ribs and yeast rolls.

Pioneer artifacts and samples of clay tiles produced in local plants are among the many interesting items on display in Brazil's Clay County Historical Museum, 100 E. National Avenue. Your Western tour also should include one or all of the thirty-two covered bridges in Parke County to the north of Brazil.

We also would suggest a visit to the quaint community of Clinton where the town's Italian heritage is artistically preserved and presented in the cuisine at Zamberletti's at the Castle restaurant. Other creative reminders of the city's Italian roots include the Quattro Stagioni Fontana or Fountain of the Four Seasons and Immigranti Piazza, a small park at 9th and Clinton streets. Another unique visitor attraction just north of Clinton is the Ernie Pyle State Historic Site at Dana, birthplace of the beloved World War II journalist. And while there, drop in the converted railroad car-restaurant, the R&R Junction at State Roads 36 and 71. If you missed seeing the covered bridges in Parke County, you will want to head north from Dana to Cayuga. About a mile north of town is the Eugene Covered Bridge built in 1873. Although no longer in use, the span is located just west of a modern concrete bridge across the Big Vermillion Creek. Or, for an effortless and picture-perfect view of the bridge we suggest you wade into some homemade pie and a catfish fiddler at the adjacent Covered Bridge Restaurant.

Nearby Attica, once a thriving port on the Wabash and Erie Canal, offers specialty shopping, dining and elegant turn-of-the-century mansions for the casual traveler. We suggest a stop at the Attica Historic Hotel or Robie's Restaurant in the central area that is undergoing revitalization efforts under the Indiana Main Street Program. Prominent among the Attica restorations is the Devon Theatre, a creatively renovated Art Deco movie house from the 1930s.

For a change of pace and a taste of urban culture and university campus attractions swing into the Greater Lafayette area where your initial visit should be at the Greater Lafayette Convention and Visitors Bureau, 301 Frontage Road, (765) 447-9999. A well-planned visit to the area would begin with a visit to their web site: www.lafayette-in.com. If Terre Haute is the capital of west central Indiana, then Lafayette/West Lafayette is the capital of the northwest central region. Our trip would include stops at the 1851-built Fowler House, a Gothic Revival mansion that now houses the Tippecanoe County Historical Museum, and a visit to the Museum of Art next door. The recently restored Tippecanoe County Court House is another architectural wonder that might appeal to your interests.

Perhaps the most unusual visitor attraction in Greater Lafayette is Wolf Park two miles north of nearby Battle Ground. There, wolves may be viewed in their natural habitat along with bison, foxes and coyote. Call ahead for information at (765) 567-2265 or visit their web site: www.wolfpark.org. We suggest an early-evening visit when the wolves are most active.

Just south of Wolf Park in the town of Battle Ground is a restful and enlightening diversion, the Tippecanoe Battlefield. There, in 1811, a confederation of Native American tribes under the direction of the Prophet attacked an encampment of U.S. soldiers under the leadership of William Henry Harrison. The defeat spelled the end of efforts by the Prophet and his brother, Tecumseh, to unify the tribes to confront American Western migration. Later, in 1840, Harrison launched his successful campaign for president of the U.S. at the site. An interpretive center provides a film presentation to visitors. Walking trails, a museum and gift shop also are located on the ninety-six-acre battle site.

Other touring tips for the western region include Greencastle, home of DePauw University. There, the nation's only publicly displayed German V-1 buzz bomb rests on the courthouse square. Also on the square is the first drug store owned by pharmaceutical giant Eli Lilly and a bank once robbed by infamous Hoosier desperado John Dillinger. Just south of the Courthouse Square on the DePauw campus is one of the Western region's most outstanding chef-operated gourmet restaurants, A Different Drummer, located in the charming Walden Inn. There, innkeeper and chef Matthew O'Neill's award-winning creations are the buzz of legions of wayfaring gourmands.

Our prescription for stress relief and an afternoon of family fun and water sports, is an outing to Monticello and the Indiana Beach Amusement Resort. Ride Indiana's first and fastest roller coaster, The Hoosier Hurricane, or enjoy a leisurely paddleboat ride on scenic Lake Shafer. For details visit their web site: www.indianabeach.com. A visit to Moe's Restaurant in Monticello, where the prime rib is Mayor Mary Walter's favorite, would be a fitting way to top off your day at Indiana Beach. Another nearby dining option popular with Purdue visitors is Solly's Restaurant at Reynolds, six miles west of Monticello.

Some visitor attractions you may not find in other tour books include:

Brook—Site of Hazelden, the English Manor-Tudor style home of Hoosier humorist, author and playwright George Ade. The colorful estate was the site of numerous parties and other large gatherings. Among the distinguished signers of the guest book were Presidents Theodore Roosevelt and William Howard Taft, and humorist Will Rogers. From Hazelden, in 1908, Taft launched his successful bid for the presidency before 25,000 supporters.

Crawfordsville—Visit the General Lew Wallace Study and Ben-Hur Museum. Completed in 1898, the domed structure now houses a museum displaying memorabilia collected by the Civil War general and statesman during his fascinating career as a military leader, author, governor of New Mexico Territory, and minister to Turkey. Designated a National Historic Landmark, it was here that Wallace wrote the epic novel, *Ben-Hur*.

Rockville—Billie Creek Village and Inn at the east edge of town is a good place to begin your Parke County tour of covered bridges and mills. A recreated pioneer village, it includes a general store, old school house, craft shops, working presentations by artisans and casual dining opportunities.

So, gas up and head out to savor the sights and hometown dining diversions of Indiana at its best . . . in the west!

For more information, contact the local visitors centers:

Monticello .... (219) 583-7220
Parke County .... (765) 569-5226
Sullivan County .... (812) 268-4836
Terre Haute .... (800) 366-3043
Tippecanoe County/
      Greater Lafayette .... (800) 872-6569

ATTICA

Restaurants nominated by Nancy Evans, councilmember

Robie's Restaurant

109 W. Main St., Attica, IN 47918
(765) 764-4351

Pork tenderloin highlights the menu at Robie's, where owner Robie Criswell is known for giving to the community. Here, she gives some of the best food at the most reasonable prices you'll find anywhere. While you're there, ask about her recent restoration and reopening of the nearby art deco movie theater, the Devon. Cash or check only. Sorry, no reservations.

Open: 11 a.m.–9 p.m. M–Th, 11 a.m.–10 p.m. F–S, closed Su

Harrison Hills Country Club

413 E. New St., Attica, IN 47918
(765) 762-2695

Enjoy the spectacular golf course view at Harrison Hills Country Club while you dine on Chef Aaron Davis' culinary creations. Councilmember Evans says the soups are outstanding and the desserts are heavenly. She suggests steak or fried chicken. Call-ahead seating for parties of five or more is available.

Open: 7 a.m.–2 p.m. daily, 5:30–8:30 p.m. F–S
MC V AmEx Di

Did you know?
The main difference between a city and a town is the separation of executive and legislative functions. A town may become a city if its population is more than 2,000.

BATTLE GROUND

Restaurants nominated by Geraldine Berghoff, clerk-treasurer

TC's Restaurant

109 N. Railroad, Battle Ground, IN 47920
(765) 567-2838

A popular meeting place for area residents, TC's is top-of-the-line according to Clerk-Treasurer Berghoff. Both the barbecued spare ribs and the chicken breast come highly recommended. Cash only. Reservations available.

Open: 5–9 p.m. T–S, 4–8 p.m. Su

Allison's Family Restaurant

103 North St., Battle Ground, IN 47920
(765) 567-4170

The hometown atmosphere makes Allison's a hit with local diners. You'll find delicious prime rib and a salad bar that draws rave reviews from just about everyone. Clerk-Treasurer Berghoff says the portions are large, so don't hesitate to ask for a doggie bag if you need it. Cash or check only. Reservations accepted for large parties.

Open: 6 a.m.–2 p.m. daily

BRAZIL

Restaurant nominated by Ken Crabb, mayor, and Jim Sheese, councilmember

Blue Bonnet

903 W. Jackson St., Brazil, IN 47834
(812) 442-1233

A local institution drawing patrons from far and wide, including Mayor Crabb and Councilmember Sheese, the Blue Bonnet's patriotic and historic decorations create a warm and healthy nonsmoking atmosphere in which to enjoy the specialties of the house, like their delicious barbecued ribs. Enjoy the homemade yeast rolls with your meal, or order some to go. No alcohol served. Reservations accepted.

Open: 7 a.m.–8 p.m. T–S, 11 a.m.–2 p.m. Su, closed M
MC V

CLINTON

Restaurant nominated by Phyllis Lambert, clerk-treasurer, Fairview Park

Zamberletti's at the Castle

1600 N. Seventh St., Clinton, IN 47842
(765) 832-8811

Exquisite Italian cuisine is the hallmark of the Castle. Clinton has been home to Zamberletti's for nine years. Golfers enjoy a great meal after a day on the nearby Matthew's Golf Course. Favorites are the garlic shrimp and chicken dinner, but anything made by the northern Italian family who owns this establishment is tempting. Weekend reservations accepted.

Open: 11 a.m.–2 p.m. T–S, 5–9 p.m. T–F,
4–9 p.m. S, 11 a.m.–3 p.m. Su, closed M
MC V Di

DANA

R&R Junction

Junction of SR 36 & 71, Dana, IN 47847
(765) 665-3010

After visiting the Ernie Pyle museum, take time to dine in a former railroad dining car. Under new management, the R&R Junction serves up home-cooked food fast and

friendly. The fish and spaghetti dishes come highly recommended. There are many menu options. Reservations accepted.

Open: 6 a.m.–2 p.m. Su–Th, 6 a.m.–9 p.m. F–S
MC V

EUGENE

The Covered Bridge Restaurant

Route 1, Eugene, IN 47928
(765) 492-7376

Located in a historic merchant's building adjacent to a covered bridge, the Covered Bridge Restaurant has been a family-owned favorite of many local and out-of-town visitors for almost a decade. Look over the display of license plates from all 50 states and many Canadian provinces while you enjoy a catfish dinner, a house specialty. And be sure to try a piece of one of their twelve homemade pies. Cash or check only, please. Sorry, no reservations.

Open: 9 a.m.–8 p.m. M–Th, 9 a.m.–9 p.m. F–S, 8 a.m.–8 p.m. Su

FLORA

Restaurants nominated by Lorna Hicks, clerk-treasurer

Creative Holidaze

206 N. Sycamore, Flora, IN 46929
(219) 967-4352

The unique gifts and floral arrangements on display at Creative Holidaze provide the perfect backdrop for the food, which includes home-baked bread at every meal. Clerk-

Treasurer Hicks recommends the fruit plate and the home-baked pies. Reservations available.

**Open: 11 a.m.–2 p.m. M–F, 5–8 p.m. third F each month,
closed S–Su
MC V AmEx**

Fisher's Restaurant

**9 W. Main St., Flora, IN 46929
(219) 967-4290**

Age can be an issue in this comfortable bar. Patrons must be over 18 or with an adult. The specials change daily at Fisher's Restaurant, where the baked tenderloin and pork filet are recommended by Clerk-Treasurer Hicks. Prime rib and fiddler's are also local favorites. The good food is made better by the excellent prices.

**Open: 10 a.m.–9 p.m. M–Th, 10 a.m.–11 p.m. F–S, closed Su
MC V**

FOWLER

Restaurants nominated by John Kuntz, town manager

100 Mile Rib & Chop House

**507 S. Grant Ave., Fowler, IN 47944
(765) 884-1906**

Located almost exactly 100 miles northwest of Indianapolis and 100 miles southeast of Chicago, the 100 Mile Rib & Chop House has been a Fowler fixture for years. Serious meat eaters will want to try the ribeye steak covered with sautéed onions and mushrooms and topped with melted mozzarella cheese, or John's "Soon to be Famous" Ribs. Fish and chicken entrées round out the menu that offers something to please just about everyone. Cash or check only, please.

Open: 11 a.m.–9 p.m. M–Th, 11 a.m.–10 p.m. F–S, 11 a.m.–1 p.m. Su

Benton County Country Club

602 W. Fourth St., Fowler, IN 47944
(765) 884-1864

A collection of signed paintings of "Impossible Holes" by Bud Chapman grace the clubhouse at the Benton County Country Club. You won't find it impossible to enjoy the golf course view while you wait for your prepared-to-order meal from the menu, which captures the best of many ethnic and regional cuisines. Town Manager Kuntz recommends the Baked Penne Veneziana.

Open: 11 a.m.–2 p.m. & 5 p.m.–8 p.m. T–Th,
5 p.m.–9 p.m. F–S, closed Su–M
MC V Di

Kidwell's Family Restaurant

117 E. Fifth St., Fowler, IN 47944
(765) 884-1700

The challenge at Kidwell's is to consume a "full" order of spaghetti, according to Town Manager Kuntz. Rumor has it that it's a tough challenge. You'll feel like you're dining alfresco with the front porch and cedar shingles inside the restaurant. And they take the "family" part of their name seriously—all nine Kidwells have worked here!

Open: 11 a.m.–2 p.m. & 4–9 p.m. M–F, 11 a.m.–8 p.m. S–Su
MC V AmEx Di

Did you know?
Indiana has 117 cities and 451 towns
for a total of 568 municipalities.

FRANKFORT

Restaurant nominated by Harold Woodruff, mayor

Pepe's

59 E. Clinton, Frankfort, IN 46041
(765) 654-9654

Begin your trip to Pepe's with a wonderful margaritta which locals swear is the "best around." This authentic Mexican restaurant is located in a historic downtown relic. In addition to cantina with dinners, Pepe's also features fresh stews. Pepe's is a two-time winner of the "Silver Platter" award in the Chicago area. Sorry, no reservations.

Open: 11 a.m.–10 p.m. Su–Th, 11 a.m.–11 p.m. F–Su
MC V AmEx Di

GREENCASTLE

Almost Home Tea Room

17 W. Franklin, Greencastle, IN 46135
(765) 653-5788

You'll feel right at home at the Almost Home Tea Room, placed daintily in Greencastle's historic downtown square. The beautiful country crafts, teas and antique amenities complement the tea room, the perfect place to enjoy a 'spot' of tea. The homemade soups, daily entrees and desserts are outstanding. The cream of broccoli soup has a national reputation for being delicious. Reservations accepted.

Open: 10 a.m.–5 p.m. M–S, 5:30–8 p.m. Th–F, closed Su
MC V Di

Hathaway's

18 S. Jackson St., Greencastle, IN 46135
(765) 653-1228

Get a little taste of Greencastle history at Hathaway's, where dishes are named after local places and events. Learn about Greencastle's past with all of the historical memorabilia. Try the Jackson Street Chicken, or any one of their delicious menu items. Weekday reservations accepted.

Open: 11 a.m.–9 p.m. M–Th, 11 a.m.–10 p.m. F–S, 11 a.m.–8 p.m. Su
MC V AmEx Di

Restaurant nominated by Michael Rokicki, councilmember

Double Decker Drive-In

1058 Indianapolis Rd., Greencastle, IN 46135
(765) 653-4302

Stop by the Double Decker Drive-In, where you can eat drive-in style or enjoy a sit-down dinner. The chicken and reuben are special favorites of Councilmember Rokicki. The broasted chicken double decker is popular, too. Banquet room available. Reservations accepted.

Open: 7 a.m.–9 p.m. daily
MC V AmEx Di

HARMONY

Restaurant nominated by Janice Gooch, councilmember

Simple Pleasures

1945 E. U.S. Hwy 40, Harmony, IN 47853
(812) 442-0101

Simple Pleasures is simply delightful, according to Councilmember Gooch. It isn't hard to relax in the casual setting while you enjoy the delicious soups, sandwiches and ice cream. Check or cash only. Sorry, no reservations.

Open: 11 a.m.–9 p.m. M–S, closed Su

Americus Restaurant

7460 State Road 25 N., Lafayette, IN 47905
(765) 589-3721

Large carved wooden animals welcome you to Americus Restaurant, where you may be a stranger when you enter but you'll immediately feel right at home. Catfish and prime rib are among the menu favorites. Clerk-Treasurer Berghoff says after one meal at Americus, you'll be sure to return for more. Reservations recommended.

Open: 10 a.m.–2 p.m. & 4:30–9:30 p.m. M–Th, 10 a.m.–2 p.m. &
4:30–10 p.m. F–S, 11:30 a.m.–9:30 p.m. Su
MC V

Did you know?
Amelia Earhart was an instructor at Purdue University and departed from Purdue Airport on her last flight.

LOGANSPORT

Restaurants nominated by Linda Klinck, councilmember

Rosemoor Emporium

989 Sherman, Logansport, IN 46947
(219) 722-4311

The menu is as varied as the antique china, but the atmosphere is consistently charming at the Rosemoor Emporium. A variety of gift items and collectibles complement the tea-room setting. Councilmember Klinck says everything on the menu is first-rate. She also suggests you leave room for one of the "always outstanding" desserts. And although the shop itself is open to all browsers and buyers, luncheon is served by reservation only. Cash or check only.

Open: 11:30 a.m.–2 p.m. T–S (food service), closed Su–M

White House Restaurant

87 S. Sixth St., Logansport, IN 46947
(219) 722-9898

You'll find breakfasts and lunches fit for a president—or at least a councilmember—at the White House Restaurant. A Logansport institution, the establishment has "been around forever," according to Councilmember Klinck. You'll feel like part of the family the minute you walk in. Cash or check only. Call-ahead seating available weekdays.

Open: 4 a.m.–1 p.m. W–S, 4–11 a.m. Su

Mr. Happy Burger

3131 E. Market St., Logansport, IN 46947
(219) 753-6418

What else would you expect but '50s décor, a soda fountain and a collection of Coke memorabilia at a joint called Mr. Happy Burger? You'll also find great pizza, chicken and country-style meals among the menu offerings. Councilmember Klinck says it's a great experience for family members of all ages.

Open: 10:45 a.m.–10 p.m. M–Th,
10:45 a.m.–11 p.m. F–S, closed Su
MC V AmEx Di

MONTICELLO

Restaurant nominated by Mary Walters, mayor

Moe's Restaurant

204 W. Rickey Rd., Monticello, IN 47960
(219) 583-5565

"Hoosier hospitality" is at its best at Moe's, where fish and chips is a specialty and the prime rib is delicious. Local folks rate it a favorite lunch spot, too. Moe will make you feel welcome when he checks to see if your meal meets with your approval. Weekend reservations recommended.

Open: 6 a.m.–9 p.m. M–F, 6 a.m.–9 p.m. S, 6 a.m.–8 p.m. Su
MC V AmEx Di

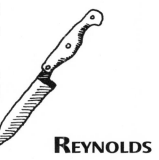

REYNOLDS

Restaurant nominated by Mary Walters, mayor, Monticello

Solly's Restaurant

U.S. 24, Reynolds, IN 47980
(219) 984-5512

Big Ten fans from Michigan and Wisconsin will vouch for the Hoosier hospitality at Solly's—a favorite spot for fans attending games at Purdue. The many out-of-state "regulars" make it often "standing room only" after a game. You can't go wrong with a steak here. Mayor Walters votes for a filet and a large Solly's salad. Weekend reservations advised.

Open: 4–9 p.m. T–Th, 4:30–10 p.m. F–S, closed Su–M
MC V

> **Did you know?**
> Two-thirds of Hoosiers live in a city or town.

WEST LAFAYETTE

Restaurants nominated by Sonya Margerum, mayor

C. Rays

401 Sagamore Parkway W., West Lafayette, IN 47906
(765) 463-2729

Relax in the casual setting at C. Rays, where a fire in the fireplace makes the atmosphere even more cozy. Mayor Margerum recommends the portobello mushroom sandwich on homemade bread or the shrimp fajita. Reservations recommended.

Open: 11 a.m.–11 p.m. M–Th, 11 a.m.–midnight F–S
MC V AmEx Di

Szechwan Garden

945 Sagamore Parkway W., West Lafayette, IN 47906
(765) 463-2364

Well-prepared Chinese food and quick service make Szechwan Garden a hit with Mayor Margerum. She recommends the moo shu pork. Another local favorite is the General Tso's chicken.

Open: 11 a.m.–9:30 p.m. M–Th, 11 a.m.–10 p.m. F–S,
noon–9 p.m. Su
MC V AmEx

Sarge Oak on Main

721 Main, West Lafayette, IN 47906
(765) 742-5230

Local folks will tell you that Sarge Oak is a main attraction. Inside the historic building you'll find mouthwatering steaks and spaghetti. Mayor Margerum recommends the filet and a slice of fresh raspberry pie. The chocolate mousse is a winner, too.

Open:h 5–9 p.m. T–Th, 5–10 p.m. F–S, closed Su–M
MC V AmEx Di

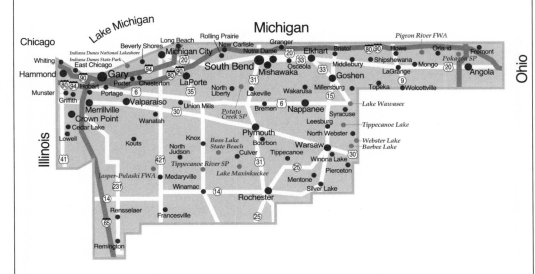

Amish culture, casinos, beaches, unique dining – best bets for experiencing Indiana's Northland!

The odds are excellent that you'll enjoy Indiana's North Country whether it's at one of the several floating casinos on Lake Michigan, an Amish educational and culinary experience or a restful walk along the scenic shores of the Dunes National Park. Indeed, the Northern Indiana borderlands offer an opportunity to "see it all." Options range from the lively gaming diversions, large art and historical museums and other urban area attractions of the western regions to the more leisurely horse-and-buggy gait of the central and eastern areas.

Take several days to savor the favorite hometown restaurants and some of the sights and sounds of this pinnacle of Indiana culture and heritage. While your starting point should be selected based on personal interests, one suggestion for a place to drop your baggage is the centrally located Elkhart area where quality lodging, dining, shopping and cultural amenities abound.

Be sure to plan time to savor all the delights at the nearby Das Dutchman Essenhaus in Middlebury, a "Top Ten" hometown restaurant in the Northern area. After you've savored the fried chicken and raspberry cream pie at the Essenhaus, we suggest a visit to the Elkhart County Visitor Center at Indiana Toll Road Exit 92 (right behind the Cracker Barrel Restaurant). Their friendly staff will provide you with driving tour maps of some of the city and county of Elkhart's hidden treasures such as the Midwest Museum of American Art where you will find large collections of Ansel Adams photographs and Norman Rockwell lithographs on display. Railroad buffs will want to visit the National New York Central Railroad Museum on Elkhart's Main Street and classic car fans should definitely wheel into the Ray Miller Auto Museum to see one of the nation's most dazzling collections of classic automobiles and vintage clothing.

The Old Bag Factory in Goshen is a charming array of shops nestled in a quaint 1896 building where artists such as quiltmakers ply their craft in full view of shoppers. And, a visit to Goshen would be a sour experience without a stop for sweets at the nationally renowned Olympia Candy Kitchen for a box of Goshen Mayor Allan Kauffman's favorite treat—chocolate covered cashews. It's a short trip from Goshen to Nappanee where a "must see" stop is Amish Acres, a restored farmstead on the National Register of Historic Places where buggy ride tours, shopping and family style "Thresher Dinners" will please thee. The restaurant gift shop usually has one of the better displays of Amish quilts.

Heading east, among your first stops should be Shipshewana and the Menno-Hof on Indiana State Road 5 where Amish and Mennonites relate the story of their heritage. While the Blue Gate Restaurant and Bakery is well worth a mealtime visit, plan to see the main attraction, the nationally-famous Shipshewana Flea Market and Auction where a thousand vendors offer everything from livestock to antiques. Hours and days of operation fluctuate so we suggest a call in advance for details: (219) 768-4129.

It's a good idea when planning to visit Amish and Mennonite operated or supported restaurants and heritage facilities to call in advance for information, especially if your visit is on a Sunday.

Now, let's hitch up our buggy and head West. A day of delicious dining in the South Bend/Mishawaka area should be paired with visits to the College Football Hall of Fame, a walk-through of the Century Center across the street, the Studebaker National Museum and, to be sure, a guided walking tour of the 155-year-old campus of the University of Notre Dame. To schedule an opportunity to experience the beauty and rich heritage of Notre Dame we suggest you call the campus Visitor Center, (219) 631-5726. Football fanatics will thrill to the interactive exhibits at the College Football Hall of Fame, and architectural aficionados will delight at the Phillip Johnson-designed Century Center, nestled on the St. Joseph River. The Century Center also houses the South Bend Regional Museum of Art. The first and last cars built by the once-thriving motor car company are among the features at the Studebaker Museum conveniently located at 525 S. Main Street. Children of all ages will enjoy the Northern Indiana Center for History, where a children's museum and Copshaholm, a Victorian Mansion, serve as the centerpieces. Exhibits also include an historical journey alongside explorers such as LaSalle, who developed the area. For details on other area attractions, call or visit the offices of the South Bend/Mishawaka Convention and Visitors Bureau, 401 E. Colfax, South Bend, (800) 282-2330.

With breathtaking views from the Lake Michigan harbor which caresses its Northern boundary, Michigan City boasts of great boating and fishing to match its dining delights along with an opportunity for great bargains at one of Indiana's finest outlet malls, Prime Outlets. Not just your average outlet mall, this well-designed facility offers a shuttle tram, and among its 120 stores such unique shopping opportunities as Burberry's and Brooks Brothers. Here too you'll find an outlet for your yen to experience the thrill of a glittering casino at the Blue Chip Casino, located, appropriately, at 2 Easy Street.

Continuing west to Gary, there are more shopping bargains to be had at the Miller Beach Shopping District on Lake Street, where local artists also display and sell their wares. After a rack of ribs and some peach cobbler at Vanzant's Ribs on the Run in Gary, stop by the Paul H. Douglas Environmental Center on Lake Street. There, interactive exhibits introduce visitors to the unique character of the area once described by poet Carl Sandburg as, "A signature of time and eternity every bit as moving as the Grand Canyon or Yosemite National Park."

More gaming thrills, excellent bargain-dining opportunities and fine accommodations entice visitors to the lakefront casinos at Gary, Hammond and East Chicago.

At Valparaiso, home of popcorn king Orville Redenbacher, opportunities for tour and dining pleasure include a must-stop at the Strongbow Inn, another Favorite Hometown Top Ten restaurant. For a restful interlude visit the nearby Chapel of the Resurrection on the Valparaiso University Campus, the largest university chapel in the world. North of town you'll find great buys at the Anderson Orchard and Winery, where the fruit wines and fresh produce lure visitors from several nearby states.

Crown Point is at the center of Lake County and was the focal point of the national news media when John Dillinger escaped from its jail by reportedly carving a pistol from a piece of wood. While Dillinger and the jail are both history, the county courthouse remains as a museum with several specialty shops. Marriage was a specialty at the Court House in yesteryears with several notables obtaining marriage licenses there. They include Rudolph Valentino, Muhammad Ali and Ronald Reagan.

You now have your license to tour and dine in this delightfully diverse area of the Hoosier State. To make sure you see all that matches your interests as well as your appetites, we suggest you contact one of the following local visitor centers:

Elkhart County/
      Northern Indiana Amish Country .... (800) 860-5949
Kosciusko County .... (800) 800-6090
LaGrange County .... (800) 254-8090
Lake County .... (800) ALL-LAKE
LaPorte County .... (800) 685-7174
Marshall County .... (800) 626-5353
Porter County .... (800) 283-8687
Steuben County .... (800) LAKE-101

ANGOLA

The Hatchery

118 S. Elizabeth St., Angola, IN 46703
(219) 665-9957

Dubbed "one of the best kept secrets" in Steuben County, The Hatchery offers diners everything from fresh seafood to tantalizing steaks. Both the filet Alaska and the sautéed soft shell crab (in season) are highly recommended. A pianist entertains diners on weekends. Nonsmoking dining room with attached lounge area. Reservations advised.

Open: 5–9 p.m. M–Th, 5–10 p.m. F–S, closed Su & holidays
MC V AmEx

CROWN POINT

Restaurant nominated by Pat DeMure, clerk-treasurer

Kelsey's Steakhouse

930 S. Court St., Crown Point, IN 46307
(219) 662-0000

Choose your own steak at Kelsey's, where the food is the best in town, according to Clerk-Treasurer DeMure. While you wait for your steak, which always is prepared to your specifications, be sure to put a generous dollop of their delicious honey butter on your bread. Attire is corporate casual. Reservations accepted.

Open: 4–9:30 p.m. M–Th, 4–10:30 p.m. F–S, noon–9:30 p.m. Su
MC V AmEx Di

CULVER

Restaurant nominated by Bobetta Washburn, clerk-treasurer

Café Max

113 S. Main St., Culver, IN 46511
(219) 842-2511

From the minute you enter this former early 1900s movie house, it's obvious Café Max is a local favorite. Memorabilia of the town, lake and Culver Military Academy grace the walls. The homemade bread, soups and omelettes come highly recommended. The sinful French toast and fresh-baked cinnamon roll served French toast style are popular, too. Stop in and relax with a hot cup of cappaccino or expresso. Sorry, no reservations.

Open: 6 a.m.–2 p.m. daily
MC V Di

ELKHART

Restaurant nominated by David Miller, councilmember

Alley Oops Diner

154 W. Hively Ave., Elkhart, IN 46517
(219) 522-0943

Take a step back in time at Alley Oops Diner where the atmosphere is delightfully reminiscent of the '60s. Get your fill of old movie star photos while you listen to the jukebox spin classic hits. The checkerboard tile floor and neon signs make your time travel complete. For a taste treat, Councilman Miller suggests the '50s burger and seasoned fries. Reservations accepted.

Open: 8 a.m.–9 p.m. M–Th, 8 a.m.–10 p.m. F–S, closed Su
MC V

Restaurants nominated by Sue Beadle, city clerk

Casey's

411 S. Main St., Elkhart, IN 46516
(219) 293-5741

One of Elkhart's oldest dining establishments, Casey's serves up excellent steaks and daily specials in a casual, relaxing atmosphere. Enjoy the Casey salad, an unusual version of a chef's salad, or Clerk Beadle's favorite, the broiled salmon filet. Reservations recommended.

Open: 11 a.m.–2p.m. & 5–11 p.m. M–S, closed Su
MC V AmEx Di

Charlie's Butcher Block

1900 Berry, Elkhart, IN 46516
(219) 264-6034

Originally a butcher shop, Charlie's Butcher Block offers up generous portions of deli-type salads and hot specials at reasonable prices for your lunchtime enjoyment. Try the pizza bread and any of the fresh baked desserts along with your lunch. Clerk Beadle recommends the Caesar, spinach, or tortellini pasta salad. And don't miss the butcher shop for a great selection of take home steaks and specialty meats.

Open: 8 a.m.–6:30 p.m. M–F, 8 a.m.–3 p.m. S
MC V AmEx Di

Lucchese's Italian Restaurant

205 E. Jackson Blvd., Elkhart, IN 46516
(219) 522-4137

Some of the tastiest Italian food in Elkhart awaits you at Lucchese's, where the homemade breads bring out the best in the meals. One of Clerk Beadle's favorites is the chicken and linguine salad. Reservations recommended.

Open: 11 a.m.–9 p.m. M–Th, 11 a.m.–10 p.m. F–S, closed Su
MC V AmEx

> **Did you know?**
> The first African-American mayor of a medium-sized city was Richard D. Hatcher, elected to the top office in Gary, a city of about 90,000, in November 1967.

GARY

Vanzant's Ribs on the Run

1907 W. 11th Ave., Gary, IN 46404
(219) 883-1429

Great old-fashioned, down-home cooking with heaping portions are what brings the locals to Vanzant's. The ribs, greens, blackeyed peas and peach cobbler come highly recommended. Be sure to check out the daily specials. Call-ahead ordering available.

Open: 11 a.m.–8 p.m. M–Th, 11 a.m.–sunset F, noon–8 p.m. Su, closed S

GOSHEN

Restaurants nominated by Allan Kauffman, mayor

Bread & Chocolate

133 S. Main St., Goshen, IN 46526
(219) 534-3053

If dessert is your favorite meal of the day, you won't want to miss Bread & Chocolate. Enjoy homemade entrees, soups and desserts ordered from the counter in the casual setting. Mayor Kauffman is especially fond of the Parmesan Chicken. The bread and specialty coffees at this European-style café speak for themselves.

Open: 8 a.m.–2 p.m. M–S, closed Su
MC V AmEx

Olympia Candy Kitchen

136 N. Main St., Goshen, IN 46526
(219) 533-5040

The aroma of candy being made in the back room makes the historic Olympia Candy Kitchen a treat for the senses. In fact, a number of U.S. presidents have sampled some of the sweet fare since the doors opened in 1912. Still owned by the same family, "the Olympia" serves up delightful meals, too. Among Mayor Kauffman's favorites are the nut olive sandwich and the homemade potato salad. Sorry, no reservations. Visit the website at www.olympiacandy.com.

Open: 7 a.m.–5 p.m. M–T & Th–F, 7 a.m.–3:30 p.m. S,
7 a.m.–12:30 p.m. Su, closed W
MC V

South Side Soda Shop

1122 S. Main St., Goshen, IN 46526
(219) 534-3790

Relax and dine in the casual, historic atmosphere of the South Side Soda Shop where the specialty sandwiches and desserts are a treat for the eyes as well as the tastebuds. Mayor Kauffman recommends the spinach salad and curly fries. Bring your checkbook, or cash only, please.

Open: 11 a.m.–8 p.m. T–S, closed Su–M

Did you know?
The sole city in Indiana and the largest city in the nation founded in this century is Gary, created in 1906. It was named for Judge Elbert H. Gary, chairman of the board at US Steel.

HAMMOND

Restaurant nominated by Helen Brown, councilmember, Munster

Phil Smidt & Sons

1205 N. Calumet Ave., Hammond, IN 46320
(219) 659-0025

A family tradition in Indiana for generations, Phil Smidt's is where the locals go when they want friendly, fast service with a variety of excellent food on the menu. Look for the dancing frog neon sign and you'll know you're in the right place. Enjoy fresh beets and bean salad while you wait for your meal. The perch and frog legs smothered in butter come highly recommended, and the chicken is outstanding, according to Councilmember Brown. Don't leave before sampling the house special dessert, gooseberry pie. Weekend reservations recommended.

Open: 11:15 a.m.–9 p.m. T–Th, 11:15 a.m.–9:30 p.m. F–S,
1–7:30 p.m. Su, closed M
MC V AmEx

Mad Vek's

6923 Calumet, Hammond, IN 46321
(219) 932-1060

One of the best parts of traveling is discovering great hole-in-the-wall dining experiences. In Hammond, it's Mad Vek's. Great hot dogs and loose meat hamburgers hit the spot, according to Councilmember Brown, who favors anything Polish from the menu. Cash only.

Open: 10:30 a.m.–8 p.m. M–F, 11 a.m.–7:30 p.m. S, closed Su

Highland

Restaurant nominated by Ronald Szafarczyk, clerk-treasurer, Griffith

Johnathon's Restaurant,
Lounge & Banquet Center

3325 Forty-fifth St., Highland, IN 46322
(219) 924-2900

According to Clerk-Treasurer Szafarczyk, the locals love Johnathon's, where seafood is one of the specialties of the house. An extensive early-bird menu offers diners choice selections, while entrees from the regular menu include soup and salad. Clerk-Treasurer Szafarczyk says it's "good food, priced right." Live entertainment highlights your experience.

Open: 3-10 p.m. T-Th, 3-11 p.m. F-S, 11 a.m.-8 p.m. Su,closed M
MC V AmEx DC

Knox

Restaurant nominated by Linda Berndt, councilmember

Ernie's Fireside Inn

907 S. Heaton St., Knox, IN 46534
(219) 772-3746

Railroad fans of all ages will love the "G" gauge train that whistles around the dining room at Ernie's. The homey, friendly atmosphere is ideal for enjoying one of the specialties of the house such as the perch sandwich or prime rib. Try the foot of onion rings, or Councilman Berndt's favorites, chicken livers and a blooming onion. Sorry, no reservations.

Open: 11 a.m.-2 p.m. & 4-9 p.m. M-Th,
11 a.m.-2 p.m. & 4-10 p.m. F-S, closed Su
MC V AmEx Di

LOWELL

Restaurant nominated by Judith Walters, clerk-treasurer

Nellie Jayne's Café

313 Commercial Ave., Lowell, IN 46356
(219) 696-6440

Peruse the array of antiques for sale while you dine in the tea room setting at Nellie Jayne's Café. The gourmet dishes characterized by generous portions, beautiful presentation and delicious taste change daily to offer diners a variety of culinary choices for breakfast and lunch. There isn't a bad choice on the menu according to Clerk-Treasurer Walters. Reservations are recommended.

Open: 7 a.m.–3 p.m. M–S, closed Su
MC V AmEx Di

Hawkeye's T'go

420 E. Commercial Ave., Lowell, IN 46356
(219) 696-5864

A hometown atmosphere and good home cooking are what make Hawkeye's T'go stand out among restaurants in Lowell's historic business district. Dine in the company of Vivian Leigh, Clark Gable and other movie stars from the '40s—or at least their likenesses. Pork tacos are the specialty of the house, and the homemade desserts will melt in your mouth. Cash only.

Open: T–F 11 a.m.–8 p.m., S noon–8p.m., Su and M closed

Did you know?
Mayors and town clerk-treasurers have the power to perform marriage ceremonies.

George's Family Restaurant

1910 E. Commercial Ave., Lowell, IN 46356
(219) 696-0313

Daily specials including a variety of Greek-American entrees are on the menu at George's, where you'll never feel rushed through a meal. From breakfast to dinner, there's something on the menu to suit everyone. Try George's omelette, the Italian beef or chicken shiskebob. Reservations accepted.

Open: 6 a.m.–9 p.m. M–S, 6 a.m.–8 p.m. Su
MC V

MERRILLVILLE

Restaurant nominated by Jim Petalas, clerk-treasurer

The Embers Restaurant

7876 Broadway, Merrillville, IN 46140
(219) 738-2242

Formerly known as The Odyssey, this father-and-son-owned restaurant boasts an expanded menu, new décor and a friendly atmosphere. This combination draws locals to The Embers, where the Greek, American and Italian cuisine gets rave reviews. Try the broiled chicken filet with rice and vegetables or the chicken lemon rice soup. Also, don't miss the homemade desserts from their bakery. Reservations accepted.

Open: 6 a.m.–11 p.m. M–Th, 6 a.m.–midnight F–S,
6 a.m.–10 p.m. Su
MC V AmEx Di

Did you know?
Merrillville is the state's most populated town, with more than 27,000 residents.

Restaurant nominated by Pat DeMure, clerk-treasurer, Crown Point

The Patio

7706 Broadway, Merrillville, IN 46410
(219) 769-7990

Greek-style pork chops highlight a menu full of out-of-this-world selections at The Patio. Crown Point Clerk-Treasurer DeMure says everything is good. Be sure to try the calamari. Weekend reservations recommended.

Open: 11 a.m.–3:30 p.m. & 4–10 p.m. M–F, 4–10 p.m. S, closed Su
MC V AmEx Di

MICHIGAN CITY

Restaurants nominated by Tom Ringo, councilmember

Basil's Restaurant

521 Franklin St., Michigan City, IN 46360
(219) 872-4500

An American bistro with a touch of Europe, Basil's offers visitors an unforgettable dining experience at a moderate price and boasts an excellent selection of food and wine. Try the terrace dining room where the glass wall begs you to watch your entree being prepared. Relax at Basil's because here they only dress up the food. This restored landmark building has its original décor restored and showcases local artists work. Call-ahead seating is available.

Open: 4:30–9 (or so) p.m. daily (*closing times vary seasonally*)
MC V AmEx Di

Lindos Restaurant

3940 Franklin St., Michigan City, IN 46360
(219) 872-0056

A good family-style restaurant with a reasonably priced menu keeps Councilmember Ringo coming back to Lindos. His favorite meal here is breakfast, which can be ordered any time. A wide variety of omelettes will meet any breakfast taste.

Open: 6 a.m.–11 p.m. daily
MC V AmEx

Swing Belly's

Lake Shore Drive at Stop 2, Michigan City, IN 46360
(219) 874-5718

You won't want to miss Swing Belly's along the beautiful Lake Michigan shoreline. Councilman Ringo says the lunch is excellent. While the nautical décor may steer you toward a fresh fish meal, the restaurant is known for its half-pound char-broiled hamburger which made Swing Belly's the hottest corner of the nearby beach. Sorry, no reservations.

Open: 11 a.m.–9 p.m. M–Th, 11 a.m.–11 p.m. F–S, noon–9 p.m. Su
MC V AmEx

MIDDLEBURY

Restaurants nominated by Lowell Miller, town manager

Muffins 'n More

109 E. Warren St., Middlebury, IN 46540
(219) 825-1566

Prepare to taste the best coffee in town at Muffins 'n More, according to Town Manager Miller. Their famous muffins include such varieties as banana carrot, chocolate fudge, morning glory, peach cobbler, pumpkin cream cheese, and sour cream pecan. The choices change daily. If you'd rather, try the quiche, a Danish or one of the other mouth-watering homemade baked goods—all reasonably priced. You can't beat the gourmet coffees and expresso drinks. Cash only.

Open: (*summer*) 7 a.m.–5 p.m., 7 a.m.–noon S
(*winter*) 7 a.m.–2 p.m. M–F, 7 a.m.–noon S
closed Su

Village Inn of Middlebury

107 S. Main St., Middlebury, IN 46540
(219) 825-2043

Treat your tastebuds to some of the finest Amish cooking around while you enjoy the display of antique kitchen items in the country-inspired atmosphere of the Village Inn of Middlebury. Folks come from all over the county to sample the fare, which includes Town Manager Miller's favorite: biscuits and gravy with potatoes. Cash or check only, please. Sorry, no reservations.

Open: 5 a.m.–8 p.m. M–Th, 5 a.m.–8:30 p.m. F, 5 a.m.–2 p.m. S,
closed Su

MONTEREY

Restaurant nominated by James C. Fleury, councilmember

"World Famous" Corner Tavern

6212 E. Main St., Monterey, IN 46960
(219) 542-9126

Just mention "World Famous" in Monterey, and you'll be sent to the corner of Main and Walnut, home of the "World Famous" Corner Tavern since 1980. Housed in a century-old building two blocks from the scenic Tippecanoe River, the restaurant features the famous "Monterey Mac" burger among its popular fare. Councilman Fleury recommends the fried chicken or steak, along with the homemade soups and veggie trays. Cash only. Reservations accepted.

Open: 7 a.m.–11 p.m. M–Th, 7 a.m.–1 a.m. F–S, closed Su

MUNSTER

Restaurant nominated by Helen Brown, councilmember

Giovanni's

603 Ridge Rd., Munster, IN 46331
(219) 836-6220

Nominated to the list of Top Ten favorite hometown restaurants in the first edition of *Indiana's Favorite Hometown Restaurants*, Giovanni's—in business for 33 years—has something to savor for anyone who loves Italian food. Popular entrees include the veal picata and the chicken vesuvio. Everything on the menu is made more delicious when accompanied by the homemade garlic rolls in the breadbasket, according to Councilmember Brown. And be sure to save room for some Grand Marnier mousse cake. Weekend reservations recommended.

Open: 11 a.m.–3 p.m. M–S, 3:30–11 p.m. M–Th,
3:30–midnight F–S, closed Su
MC V AmEx

NAPPANEE

Amish Acres Restaurant

1600 West Market, US 6 W, Nappanee, IN 46550
(219) 773-4188 *or call tollfree* **(800) 800-4942**

No trip to north-central Indiana is complete without a visit to Amish Acres to learn about Indiana's Amish culture, and no visit is complete without a fulfilling stop at its fine and expansive restaurant. There, waitresses in historical garb have served their famous fried chicken, bean soup and their award winning shoo-fly pie since 1971. Ample parking is available immediately south of the restaurant. After eating, browse the gift shop for homemade breads and noodles, or perhaps an Amish quilt. Sorry, no reservations. Open from March 1– December 30.

Open: 11 a.m.–7 p.m. M–S, 11 a.m.–6 p.m. Su
MC V Di

NORTH MANCHESTER

Restaurant nominated by Nancy Reed, clerk-treasurer

Mr. Dave's

102 E. Main St., North Manchester, IN 46962
(219) 982-4769

For an award-winning hand-breaded tenderloin, it doesn't get any better than Mr. Dave's, which was featured in the November 1998 issue of Indianapolis Monthly magazine as Indiana's best tenderloin. For another tasty option, Clerk-Treasurer Reed recommends the bar-be-que pork sandwich, old-fashioned onion rings and yogurt of the day. When the weather allows, enjoy your meal outside under the umbrellas. Cash or local checks only, please.

Open: *(April–December)* **10 a.m.–8 p.m. M–S,**
(January–March) **10 a.m.–3 p.m. M–Th, 10 a.m.–8 p.m. F–S**
closed Su

Did you know?
The main difference between a city and a town is the separation of executive and legislative functions. A town may become a city if its population is more than 2,000.

ORLAND

Wall Lake Tavern

6100 N. 1200 East Wall Lake, Orland, IN 46776
(219) 829-6335

Knotty pine and rustic accessories bring a taste of the great outdoors in, to give the Wall Lake Tavern old-fashioned appeal. The stuffed walleye is a favorite at the tavern, and the baked or fried walleye and fresh cut steaks are good choices. Delicious homemade soups, a fresh salad bar, and gourmet coffees are served fast and friendly at the Wall Lake Tavern. Cash only, please. Reservations available.

Open: 11 a.m.–9 p.m. T–Th, 11 a.m.–10 p.m. F–S, noon–8 p.m. Su, closed M

OSCEOLA

Restaurant nominated by Donna Reinholtz, clerk-treasurer

Between the Buns

1720 Lincolnway, Osceola, IN 46561
(219) 679-4474

Sports is the name of the game at Between the Buns, where fans over age 21 can enjoy mountains of memorbilia, the latest sporting event on television and a vast array of creatively named entrees. Try the Larry Birdwich, a charbroiled boneless fresh chicken breast, or the Ryne Sandburger, a burger topped with sauteed onions, mushrooms and smothered with melted Monterey Jack and cheddar cheeses. For a championship meal, Clerk-Treasurer

Reinholtz recommends the Bob Griese Burger on rye with grilled onions and The Greens with homemade sweet and sour dressing. Reservations accepted. Visit them ahead of time at www.betweenthebuns.com.

Open: 11 a.m.–midnight M–S, noon–midnight Su
MC V AmEx Di

PLYMOUTH

Restaurants nominated by Jack Greenlee, mayor

The Brass Rail

225 N. Michigan, Plymouth, IN 46563
(219) 936-7004

Located in the heart of downtown Plymouth, The Brass Rail offers diners one mouth-watering temptation after another in a casual atmosphere. Fresh seafood Alfredo and hand-breaded cod highlight the menu. For a taste of the best, Mayor Greenlee recommends the sauteed lake perch. Reservations recommended.

Open: 11 a.m.–10 p.m. M–Th, 11 a.m.–10:30 p.m. F–S
MC V AmEx Di

Christo's

2227 N. Michigan St., Plymouth, IN 46563
(219) 935-5100

Choose from a variety of American, Greek and Mexican entrees at Christo's, where casual, family dining in a clean, comfortable setting is the name of the game. Try the mayor's favorite dish, chicken breast with asparagus, and be sure to leave room for a piece of homemade pie or cake. Reservations accepted.

Open: 6 a.m.–midnight daily
MC V

The Hayloft

West Jefferson St., Plymouth, IN 46563
(219) 936-6680

Antiques and photos of old barns highlight the walls at The Hayloft, a 100-year-old rustic red barn converted into a restaurant. Diners can choose from 30 entrees, including prime rib and buffalo steak. For a different appetizer, try the alligator hors d'oeuvres. And ask about "Homer"—the ghost the restaurant staff has named. Call-ahead seating is available.

Open: 4:30–9 p.m. M–Th, 4:30–10 p.m. F–S,
seasonal hours Su (*call*)
MC V AmEx Di

PORTER

Restaurants nominated by Charlene Hauber, clerk-treasurer

Wagner's

361 Wagner Rd., Porter, IN 46304
(219) 926-7614

For out-of-this-world ribs that simply melt in your mouth, head for Wagner's. Relax in the family-friendly atmosphere, and don't be afraid to lick your fingers! The ribs don't come any better. It's just plain "good food" Clerk-Treasurer Hauber says. Sorry, no reservations.

Open: 10 a.m.–11 p.m. M–S, noon–10 p.m. Su
MC V AmEx

Santiago's

124 Lincoln Ave., Porter, IN 46304
(219) 926-6518

Tempt your tastebuds with the sizzle of Mexican food at Santiago's, where the food and prices are good and the atmosphere couldn't be friendlier. Clerk-Treasurer Hauber says to try the wet burrito or the enchiladas suizas. Weekend reservations recommended.

Open: 11 a.m.–9 p.m. Su–Th, 11 a.m.–10 p.m. F–S
MC V

RENSSELAER

Restaurants nominated by Susan Smith, mayor

City Office & Pub

114 S. Van Rensselaer St., Rensselaer, IN 47978
(219) 866-9916

Politicians and business leaders alike favor the City Office & Pub, with its display of historical pictures, antiques and political memorbilia. Located just across from the courthouse, the restaurant offers a variety of daily homemade soup and sandwich luncheon specials. Dinner selections include their Pub Burger and blackened salmon. Mayor Smith prefers the seafood and prime rib.

Open: 11 a.m.–9 p.m. T–Th, 11 a.m.–10 p.m. F–S, closed Su–M
MC V Di

Daryl's Pastry Shop

110 W. Washington St., Rensselaer, IN 47978
(219) 866-7883

Located on the town square, Daryl's Pastry Shop is famous for its pastries, cakes, cookies and pies. Daily luncheon specials highlight the menu. Mayor Smith recommends the chicken salad sandwich and cream roll or apple fritter, and she says the brownies are excellent.

Open: 4:30 a.m.–2 p.m. M–T, 4:30 a.m.–3 p.m. W,
5 a.m.–10 p.m. Th, 4:30 a.m.–4 p.m. F,
4:30 a.m.–1 p.m. S, 5 a.m.–8 p.m. Su
MC V AmEx Di

Devon's Family Restaurant

732 S. College Ave., Rensselaer, IN 47978
(219) 866-7153

Friends and families meet at Devon's, where good food and service are always the case. Located in College Square Mall, the restaurant offers a Wednesday night pasta buffet, a Friday night seafood buffet, and Sunday brunch. The barbecued ribs and broasted chicken are tasty, too. Weekend reservations available.

Open: 7 a.m.–9 p.m. Su–Th, 7 a.m.–10 p.m. F–S
MC V

SCHERERVILLE

Restaurant nominated by Pat DeMure, clerk-treasurer, Crown Point

Teibel's

1775 Route 41, Schererville, IN 46375
(219) 865-2000

Area residents have come to Teibel's for generations to enjoy the buttered lake perch, fried chicken and frog legs in a relaxed, casual atmosphere. Great fish is what has made the restaurant stand out in Crown Point Clerk-Treasurer DeMure's opinion. The stuffed mushrooms come highly recommended. Reservations recommended.

Open: 11 a.m.–10 p.m. Su–Th, 11 a.m.–11 p.m. F–S
MC V AmEx

TOPEKA

Restaurant nominated by DeWayne Bontrager, clerk-treasurer

Tiffany's

414 East Lake, Topeka, IN 46751
(219) 593-2988

Warm hospitality and simply delicious home cooking go hand-in-hand at Tiffany's, where you can order from the menu, or dine family-style or from the smorgasboard. The atmosphere is casual, smoke-free and the prices are just right. Clerk-Treasurer Bontrager recommends the Swiss Steak dinner and the homemade pies. Friday and Saturday buffets offer a changing array of chicken, roast beef, shrimp and barbecue ribs. Reservations accepted weekdays.

Open: (*summer*) **6 a.m.–8 p.m. M, 6 a.m.–9 p.m. T–S**
(*winter*) **6 a.m.–7 p.m. M, 6 a.m.–8 p.m. T–S**
MC V AmEx Di

TOWN OF PINES

Restaurant nominated by Larry Fleck, clerk-treasurer

Pumps on 12

3085 W. Dunes Hwy, Town of Pines, IN 46360
(219) 874-6201

Seafood and steak are the specialties of the house at Pumps on 12. The early roadhouse atmosphere takes you back in time while you enjoy such specialties as the New York strip sirloin, beef-kebab, fresh walleye pike or red snapper. The reasonably priced entrees include soup or salad, potato or vegetable, rolls, and coffee or tea.

Open: 11 a.m.–10 p.m. M–Th, 11 a.m.–10:30 p.m. F–S
noon–9 p.m. Su (winter hours vary)
MC V AmEx

SHIPSHEWANA

Restaurants nominated by Norm Kauffmann, town manager

The Blue Gate Restaurant & Bakery

195 N. Van Buren St., Shipshewana, IN 46565
(219) 768-4725

Enjoy the best of traditional Amish cooking served family-style or order from the menu at The Blue Gate. Browse any of the shops in Riegsecker Marketplace while you wait for your table, then prepare to delight your tastebuds with made-from-scratch specialties including chicken, ham or roast beef accompanied by mashed potatoes, gravy, and an array of vegetables. Town Manager Kauffmann recommends Mel's Favorite, a charbroiled chicken breast served with a smashed baked potato, topped with steamed vegetables, cheese sauce and bacon bits. And we haven't even mentioned the desserts! Call-ahead seating is available.

Open: 7 a.m.–8 p.m. M–S, closed Su
MC V Di

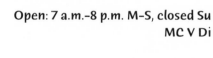

Country Corral Restaurant

260 E. N. Village Dr., Shipshewana, IN 46565
(219) 768-4589

Dine in this casual diner where the menu features a variety of soups and sandwiches. Local workers like to keep this one to themselves because of the daily specials and homeade pies. Cash or checks only. Reservations accepted.

Open: 5 a.m.–2 p.m. M–S, closed Su

Buggy Wheel Buffet

160 N. Morton St., Shipshewana, IN 46565
(219) 768-4444

Amish cooking highlights the ample lunch and dinner offerings at the Buggy Wheel Buffet, where you won't leave hungry. Indulge on their famous stuffing dressing and homemade noodles, but be sure to leave room for dessert! A breakfast menu is also available. Cash or checks only, please. Reservations accepted for large parties. The Buggy Wheel is not open in the month of January.

Open: *(May–Oct.)* **11 a.m.–7 p.m. M & Th–F, 7 a.m.–7 p.m. T–W & S,**
(Nov.–Apr.) **11 a.m.–7 p.m. F, 7 a.m.–7 p.m. S,**
closed Su

SOUTH BEND

Restaurants nominated by Steve Luecke, mayor

The LaSalle Grill

115 W. Colfax, South Bend, IN 46602
(219) 288-1155

If you get a sense of a bygone age upon entering The LaSalle Grill, don't be surprised. The restaurant is located in a historic building that once housed a hotel and a men's clothing store. Unique menu items feature hardwood-grilled steak and game, including ostrich and caribou. Be sure to try the warm focaccia and olive oil brought to your table when you are seated. Appropriate attire is corporate casual (no jeans or tennis shoes, please). Reservations accepted on weekends. Visit this establishment on the Web at www.lasallegrill.com.

Open: 5–10 p.m. M–Th, 5–11 p.m. F–S, closed Su
MC V AmEx Di

East Bank Emporium Restaurant

121 S. Niles Ave., South Bend, IN 46617
(219) 234-9000

Ask for a seat with a view of the scenic St. Joseph River at the East Bank Emporium, located in the 1912 Emporium Building overlooking the St. Joseph River and the Century Center convention facility. Let the chicken pita for lunch or Steak Neptune at dinner dazzle your tastebuds as you relax in the casual atmosphere. Reservations recommended.

Open: 11 a.m.–3 p.m. & 5–10 p.m. M–F,
11 a.m.–3 p.m. & 5–11 p.m. S, 4–9 p.m. Su
MC V AmEx Di CB DC

Sunny Italy Café

601 N. Niles Ave., South Bend, IN 46617
(219) 232-9620

Generations of families dine at the Sunny Italy Café, which boasts an atmosphere just like "sunny" Italy. Dine in the casual setting where flavorful dishes include homemade pasta, spaghetti and homemade meatballs, pan fried chicken and homemade pies. Try the garlic spaghetti for a real treat. Reservations and call-ahead seating available.

Open: 4:30–10 p.m. W–S, closed Su–T
MC V

Valparaiso

Restaurants nominated by David Butterfield, mayor

Restaurante don Quijote

119 E. Lincolnway, Valparaiso, IN 46383
(219) 462-7976

Food is anything but ordinary at don Quijote, billed as Indiana's only authentic Spanish restaurant. You won't find tacos or burritos on the menu; instead you will find an adventure in dining that mixes the best of Greek, Middle Eastern and French influences. Specialties include Paella Marinera, a traditional shellfish and saffron rice dish including jumbo shrimp, flounder, clams, mussels, squid and crab legs, or Mayor Butterfield's favorite, Pinchos Morunos, Moorish style skewered veal and pork marinated in wine, paprika, oregano, parsley, garlic and olive oil. Watch for information about an occasional wild game buffet, too. Reservations advised.

Open: 11:30 a.m.–2:30 p.m. M–F, 5–9:30 p.m. M–Th,
5–11 p.m. F–S, closed Su
MC V DC

Clayton's

66 W. Lincolnway, Valparaiso, IN 46383
(219) 531-0612

Named one of the top ten nonsmoking restaurants in the Chicago metropolitan area, Clayton's combines the best in elegant dining with simple Midwestern friendliness. Located in a turn-of-the-century storefront just off Valparaiso's main square, Clayton's leaves no detail to chance in the presentation of its outstanding continental cuisine. Mayor

Butterfield recommends the rack of lamb, and any of the outstanding appetizers and original soups. Reservations recommended, especially on weekends.

Open: 5–9 p.m. T–Th, 5–10:30 p.m. F–S,
3–7:30 p.m. Su, closed M
MC V AmEx Di

WARSAW

ViewPoint Restaurant

2519 E. Center St., Warsaw, IN 46580
(219) 269-1001

The house specialty at ViewPoint Restaurant is prime rib, and from the locals' point of view the lobster and pasta are tops. Breakfast is served on Saturdays. There also is a scrumptious Sunday brunch. Reservations advised.

Open: 11 a.m.–2 p.m. & 5–10 p.m. M–S, 7–10:30 a.m. S,
8 a.m.–2 p.m. & 5–8 p.m. Su
MC V AmEx

WHITING

Restaurant nominated by Robert Bercik, mayor

Dimitri's Cake & Steak House

1342 119th St., Whiting, IN 46394
(219) 659-1390

You may have to share a seat with a Chicago resident at this regional favorite. The more than 100 menu items ensures something for everyone, including steak, seafood and chicken fixed a variety of ways. Vegetable lasagna and pastas are on the menu for vegetarians. Be sure and save room for the chocolate cheesecake or Oreo cake.

Open: 6 a.m.–10 p.m. M–S, 6 a.m.–9 p.m. Su
MC V AmEx DC

What's Cookin'

1950 Indianapolis Blvd., Whiting, IN 46394
(219) 659-3426

A trip to What's Cookin' will send you right back to the 1930s. The causual restaurant serves breakfast, but is known for its ham and eggs and chili which are served up all day. Sorry, no reservations.

Open: 5 a.m.–3 p.m. daily
MC V

Did you know?
Elected officials at the local level provide many of our most critical services such as utilities, roads, police, and fire protection.

EASTERN

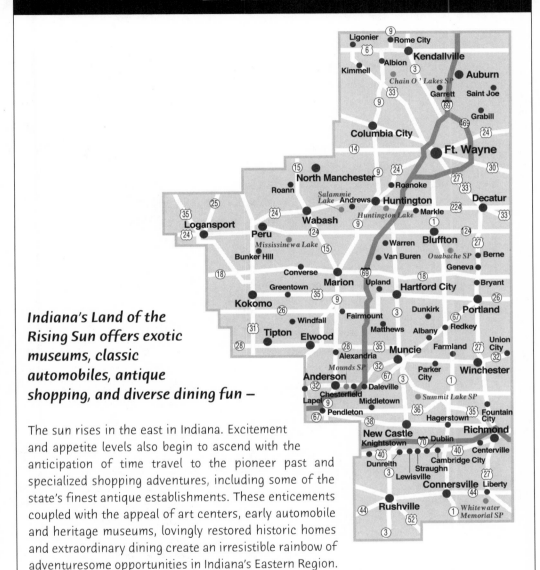

Indiana's Land of the Rising Sun offers exotic museums, classic automobiles, antique shopping, and diverse dining fun –

The sun rises in the east in Indiana. Excitement and appetite levels also begin to ascend with the anticipation of time travel to the pioneer past and specialized shopping adventures, including some of the state's finest antique establishments. These enticements coupled with the appeal of art centers, early automobile and heritage museums, lovingly restored historic homes and extraordinary dining create an irresistible rainbow of adventuresome opportunities in Indiana's Eastern Region.

Eastern Indiana is the home of such notables as the late actor James Dean, the current cartoon character Garfield the Cat, Johnny Appleseed, and former Vice President Dan Quayle. Hoosier heroes of the court and gridiron are enshrined here, too, at New Castle's Indiana Basketball Hall of Fame and at Richmond's Indiana Football Hall of Fame.

Here, too, you will find some of the world's most glamorous classic automobiles. More than 140 vintage, antique, and special interest motor vehicles are on glorious display at the Auburn-Cord-Dusenberg Museum, located in the original Auburn Motor Car Company building in Auburn. The rich auto-making heritage of Connersville, Kokomo, and Richmond also are preserved and displayed.

Modern auto travel in the Eastern region is effortless and scenic. Whether your visit is anchored in the urban areas of Anderson/Muncie, Marion, Fort Wayne, Kokomo, New Castle or Richmond, convenient accessibility is provided via Interstates 69 and 70 or U.S. 24, 30 and 31. Four special tour guides of the region using these roads are available by calling (800) 828-8414. One suggestion is to plan a day or two in the Richmond area to visit attractions in the southern section of the region. Another day might be spent at Marion or the Anderson/Muncie area and, finally, several days to explore the fascinations of the greater Fort Wayne region to the North. Numerous bed and breakfast inns and traditional lodging with a wide range of prices are available in these locations by contacting the appropriate convention/visitor bureaus. We believe you will find your visit will be met with much more enthusiasm in the less-traveled communities than the more publicized traditional tourist stops. Thus, we have focused on some of these hidden treasures in this piece.

Family fun opportunities abound at such centers as Bryant's Bearcreek Farm, a two-hundred-acre spread offering dining, amusement rides, lodging and a theatre. Call (800) 288-7630 for details. Near Geneva is Amishville USA where you may tour an Amish home, ride a buggy and view a working gristmill. Call (219) 589-3536 for more information. And kids will do somersaults of appreciation after a visit to the Circus City, Peru. There the Miami County Museum, 51 N. Broadway, offers exhibits which include circus memorabilia and details on the days when Peru served as the winter headquarters for several circuses. Call (765) 473-9183 for show times. A first stop when visiting the Circus City is their web site, www.miamicountyin.com, which includes information on the July Circus City festival, it's www.perucircus.com. The musically inclined will want to take Peru's Cole Porter walking tour, which includes his birthplace, 102 E. 3d Street. Porter, was born in 1891, fought with the French in World War I and wrote numerous Broadway musicals and individual songs, including the classics "Begin the Beguine" and "In the Still of the Night."

If you're just horsing around, then you'll want to visit Indiana's only pari-mutuel race track, Hoosier Park at Anderson for an afternoon or evening of thoroughbred or harness racing. For post times, call (800) 526-RACE. An unusual attraction at Anderson is the Historical Military Armor Museum, 2330 Crystal Street, where the displays include tanks and other military vehicles from World War II to present. For details call (765) 649-TANK. Old theatre buffs will marvel at the quality of the restoration of the Paramount Theatre, 1124 Meridian Plaza. For special event information, call (800) 523-4658.

Among the hundreds of visitor attractions in Fort Wayne, one stands tall—the Lincoln Museum, 200 E. Berry Street. It is a must-see attraction in the state's second largest city. It's huge. Indeed, the museum provides the largest public viewing of Lincoln memorabilia. Eighteen interactive touchscreen computer stations and eleven exhibit galleries and four theaters provide visitors with a full picture of the life and deeds of the Great Emancipator. Details on the museum as well as other Fort Wayne attractions are available via the web site of the Fort Wayne Convention and Visitors Bureau: www.fwcvb.org.

In Richmond you will find a true hidden treasure in the Wayne County Historical Museum, 1150 N. A Street, where the expansive facility offers displays one would expect in much larger communities. Among the more popular exhibits is the mummy of an Egyptian princess, a 1929 Davis airplane, antique autos and artifacts from the pioneer era and early jazz recording industry that once flourished in this Quaker-settled community. Among the more unusual displays is an outstanding collection of Native American pottery and basketry, including some outstanding examples of ancient Anasazi craftwork. Most recently the museum has received a collection of unpublished photographic plates of the early work of famous aviation pioneers, the Wright Brothers, who once lived nearby. In the undiscovered treasure category is the Garr Mansion, which has been called one of the top museum homes in the nation. Built in 1876, the hillside house was restored in the 1970s by fifth-generation descendent Joanna Mikesell with the original furnishings. Call for tour details, (765) 966-7184. Another popular area attraction is "Antique Alley," on the scenic National Road (U.S. 40) west of the city. This antique shopper's paradise displays an array of more than nine hundred antique dealers, spanning thirty-three miles. Items offered range from Civil War relicts to Willet cherry furniture. One establishment, Webb's, four miles west of Richmond at Centerville, claims to be the world's largest antique mall with quality items on display. Any stop in Centerville must include a mealtime visit to Jag's Café, where the back bar is an antique from the 1893 World's Fair. We heartily recommend an extended visit to this undiscovered community. For suggestions to match your interest, we recommend an exploratory stop at the Old National Road Visitor Center, 5701 National Road, east of Richmond. Call Rhonda or Dale at the center, (800) 828-8414 or, prior to your visit, drop in on the web site of the Richmond/Wayne County Convention and Visitors Bureau at www.visitrichmond.org.

Another community missing from many tour books is Muncie, home of Ball State University where comedian Dave Letterman earned a degree and continues to endow scholarships and other worthwhile programs. A must-see sight at Muncie is the Minnetrista Cultural Center and Oakhurst Gardens, 1200 Minnetrista Parkway, where regional art, interactive historic exhibits, and garden tours will help you work up an appetite. And, you should pounce on an opportunity to visit Garfield The Cat at the Muncie Children's Museum, 515 High Street. Here, the younger members of your party can learn about cartooning at Garfield's first and only permanent exhibit. Call (765) 286-1660 for details.

Kokomo is another yet-to-be nationally discovered jewel for those weary of mainstream attractions. Automotive history buffs will thrill at the City of Firsts Automotive Heritage Museum and the Elwood Haynes Museum. It was Elwood Haynes who in 1894 designed and drove down Pumpkinvine Pike America's first commercially built gasoline-powered automobile. In all fifteen major discoveries and inventions are claimed to have taken place in Kokomo. The Haynes Museum, 1915 S. Webster Street, is located in the former two-story brick home of the automobile pathfinder where visitor attractions include a 1905 Model L Haynes automobile. Next door is the Kokomo Art Association's gallery. An off-the-beaten-path opportunity is provided by the Kokomo Opalescent Glass Co., 1310 S. Market Street, where factory tours may be followed by a visit to their gift shop. Call (765) 457-1829 for more information. The Greentown Glass Museum, eight miles east of Kokomo on State Road 22, offers displays of collector's glass made around the turn of the century. Call (765) 628-6206 for details.

It is, however, the smaller communities and scenic rural backroads where some of the more appealing Favorite Hometown Restaurants and visitor attractions are nestled. For a nostalgic tour of a few more fascinating places, drop in on historic downtown Connersville and hop aboard the Whitewater Valley Railroad's thirty-two-mile scenic ride through the Whitewater Valley to Metamora, an historically recreated canal town with more than a hundred shops and a working grist mill. Call (765) 395-3256 for details.

Wabash, too, merits the time and attention of the discriminating traveler. The Honeywell Center, 275 W. Market Street, offers diverse cultural and recreational facilities including Eugenia's Restaurant, Clark Art Gallery, and Ford's Theatre. Call (800) 626-6345 for details.

As the sun sets, we hope your senses have feasted on the best of the hometown dining and recreational pleasures in Indiana's eastern tourism region. For more information, conatct the local visitors centers below:

Anderson/Madison County .... (800) 533-6569
Fort Wayne/Allen County .... (800) 767-7752
Huntington County .... (800) 848-4282
Kokomo/Howard County .... (800) 837-0971
Ligonier Visitors Bureau .... (800) 417-3562
Marion/Grant County .... (800) 662-9474
Muncie Visitors Bureau .... (800) 568-6243

ALBANY

Restaurants nominated by Marita Fields, clerk-treasurer

Osborn's Restaurant

220 W. State St., Albany, IN 47320
(765) 789-8281

The locals like to meet at Osborn's where the home-style meals are priced just right. You'll love the bean soup and cornbread, and don't leave without trying a piece of their fantastic pie. Cash or check only. Sorry, no reservations.

Open: 5 a.m.–7 p.m. M–F, 5 a.m.–1:30 p.m. S, closed Su

Pete's Duck Inn

721 State St., Albany, IN 47320
(765) 789-8488

Breaded tenderloins and fried chicken top the list of recommended dishes at Pete's Duck Inn. Known for its friendly service and great food, this is where the locals meet and socialize. Clerk-Treasurer Fields recommends the pork chops and nachos. Cash only. Reservations recommended on weekends.

Open: 8 a.m.–10 p.m. M–F, 9 a.m.–11 a.m. S, noon–8 p.m. Su

ANDERSON

Restaurant nominated by J. Mark Lawler, mayor

Lucy's

2460 East County Road 67, Anderson, IN 46017
(765) 643-3144

Mayor Lawler likes to frequent Lucy's for a hearty country breakfast while he catches up on the latest happenings and takes advice on how to run the city from the "regulars." His favorite is a special breakfast platter of eggs, sausage, bacon, potatoes, and toast. The country pot roast and homemade chicken and noodle dinners get the top votes from His Honor, too. Banquet room available. Cash only. Reservations accepted.

Open: 6 a.m.–9 p.m. M–S, 6 a.m.–3 p.m. Su

AUBURN

Restaurant nominated by Norman Rohm, mayor

Bread Basket

115 N. Main St., Ste. 201, Auburn, IN 46706
(219) 925-4257

You'll find unbelievably tasty baked goods and outstanding daily luncheon specials amid the antiques and quaint country atmosphere at the Bread Basket, located on the second floor in Auburn's historic downtown district. Mayor Rohm says all the sandwiches are exceptional. The ham and cheese quiche is a hit with visitors from all around. Cash or check only. Reservations accepted for parties of six or more.

Open: 9 a.m.–5 p.m. M–F, 10 a.m.–2 p.m. S, closed Su

Ambrosia

207 Touring Dr., Auburn, IN 46706
(219) 927-1422

Exceptionally large portions ensure that you won't go away hungry from Ambrosia. Expect a tableside visit from the owners to make sure of it. A variety of foods including Greek selections to tempt diners. The gyros and lasagna both draw rave reviews. Reservations available for large parties.

Open: 5 a.m.–11 p.m. M–Th, 5 a.m.–midnight F–S,
6 a.m.–10 p.m. Su
MC V AmEx Di

AVILLA

Restaurant nominated by Paul Shepherd, councilmember; DeWayne Bontrager, clerk-treasurer, Topeka; and Jennie DePaolo, clerk-treasurer, Garrett

St. James Restaurant

204 E. Albion St., Avilla, IN 46710
(219) 897-2114

A renovated historic hotel built in 1878 houses the St. James Restaurant, which remains in operation by the William Freeman family who converted the hotel into a restaurant in 1949. You'll want to get a look at the beautiful hand-carved wood at the bar. The cozy atmosphere offers the perfect setting for enjoying the house specialties: chicken, fish and steaks. Councilman Shepherd suggests the Cajun ribeye steak. Reservations accepted weekdays.

Open: 7 a.m.–10 p.m. M–Th, 7 a.m.–11 p.m. F–S, closed Su
MC V

CENTERVILLE

Jag's Café

129 East Main St., Centerville, IN 47330
(765) 855-2282

Jag's Café offers delightful dining in a unique atmosphere featuring antiques, including the bar and back bar from the 1895 Chicago World's Fair, and numerous autographed guitars and photos of contemporary stars. Local officials recommend you try one of the house specialties: French onion soup. Don't miss the cheesecake—guaranteed to satisfy your sweet tooth! Reservations advised.

Open: 11 a.m.–9 p.m. T–Th & Su, 11 a.m.–11 p.m. F–S, closed M
MC V Di

CONNERSVILLE

Restaurants nominated by Marion Newhouse, mayor

Great Expectations
Restaurant & Catering

126 E. Fourth St., Connersville, IN 47331
(765) 825-0911
3542 N. Western Ave., Connersville, IN 47331
(765) 827-9993

Immerse yourself in beautiful historic architecture when you dine at Great Expectations on Fourth St., located in one of Connersville's older homes, renovated specifically for the restaurant. You'll find many of the vegetables home-grown by the owners. Mayor Newhouse suggests the tuna or chicken salad. Reservations are helpful, but not necessary.

Open: (*both locations*) 11 a.m.–2 p.m. M–F, 5–9 p.m. F–S,
closed Su
MC V

The Willows

522 N. Central Ave., Connersville, IN 47331
(765) 825-5552

Local history abounds at The Willows, where Mayor Newhouse recommends the deli bar. It features soups, salads and cold cut sandwiches. Diners may choose from daily dinner specials including Monday's all-you-can-eat catfish and Friday's seafood buffet, or any of the tempting menu offerings.

Open: 8 a.m.–2 p.m. M–F, 5–9 p.m. M–Th, 4:30–9 p.m. F,
5–9 p.m. S, closed Su
MC V AmEx

Nibbler's Nook

3201 N. Waterloo Rd., Connersville, IN 47331
(765) 825-5906

The locals love to head to Nibbler's Nook for early morning breakfasts. Large servings of the delicious home cooking keep them coming back for lunch. Mayor Newhouse recommends the bean soup and cornbread. He also suggests you try a side of fried potatoes. Cash only.

Open: 5 a.m.–2 p.m. M–S, 5–11 a.m. Su

CONVERSE

Restaurants nominated by J. R. Hodson, councilmember

Herschbergers Essen Haus

223 N. Jefferson, Converse, IN 46919
(765) 395-5905

Everything about Herschbergers speaks to its Amish heritage. Its Amish owners have decorated and staffed this locale for authentic meals. You won't want to miss the homemade pies, bread, and noodles. Chicken is the specialty, but outstanding fish is served on Fridays. Cash only.

Open: 6 a.m.–8 p.m. M–S, closed Su

Marty's Pub

304 N. Jefferson St., Converse, IN 46919
(765) 395-5442

Opened in 1936, Marty's features a large family room separate from the pub for family dining. Tempt your

tastebuds with an array of specialty sandwiches. Steak lovers take note: each steak is custom cut and cooked to your order, then served with steak fries and a salad.

**Open: 11 a.m.–10 p.m. T–Th, 11 a.m.–11 p.m. F, noon–11 p.m. S,
4 - 10 p.m. Su, closed M
MC V AmEx**

DENVER

Restaurant nominated by Mary Titus, clerk-treasurer

Denver Café

**17 Payson St., Denver, IN 46926
(765) 985-2040**

Savor small-town Indiana at its best at the Denver Café, where even the employees keep coming back from retirement to work. You'll love the family atmosphere almost as much as the broasted chicken and deviled pork steak, according to Clerk-Treasurer Titus. The dining room is open Thursday–Saturday, but you can get carry-out any night. Cash only.

Open: 5–9 p.m. Th–S *(dining room)*

DECATUR

Restaurant nominated by Fred Isch, mayor, John Schultz, councilmember

West End Restaurant

**702 W. Monroe St., Decatur, IN 46733
(219) 724-2938**

You'll wonder whose mom is in the kitchen when you taste the fried chicken and potatoes and gravy at the West End. Believed to be the oldest restaurant in Decatur, the establishment opened in 1897 and once marked the west side of the city. Mayor Isch says you can't go wrong with the hand dipped and battered onion rings. Don't ask for the batter recipe, though, it's a secret. Cash or check only please.

Open: 5:30 a.m.-7 p.m. M-T, 5:30 a.m.-9 p.m. W-Th,
5:30 a.m.-10 p.m. F, 6 a.m.-10 p.m. S, closed Su

Restaurant nominated by Fred Isch, mayor

The Galley

622 N. 13th St., Decatur, IN 46733
(219) 724-8181

Known for its "famous fish," The Galley has some of the friendliest service around, according to Mayor Isch. From the nautical theme to the outstanding menu selection, it is obvious that this is no ordinary fish restaurant. His Honor recommends Galley's fish dinner and coleslaw. Other selections include mahimahi and salmon steak. The fresh seafood and reasonable prices make The Galley perfect for the entire family.

Open: 10:30 a.m.-9 p.m. M-Th, 10:30 a.m.-103 p.m. F-S,
10:30 a.m.-8 p.m. Su
MC V

EATON

The Mississinewa Tavern

125 West Harris St., Eaton, IN 47338
(765) 396-9371

Get a taste of Mexico at The Mississinewa Tavern, which features Wednesday-night taco and taco salad specials. Food's good the rest of the week, too. It's a popular local favorite. Sorry, no reservations and no credit cards.

Open: 7:30 a.m.-midnight M-Th, 7:30 a.m.-1 a.m. F,
8 a.m.-1 a.m. S, noon-8 p.m. Su

ECONOMY

Restaurant nominated by Norma Mosier, clerk-treasurer

Kopper Kettle

13602 US Hwy 35 S, Economy, IN 47339
(765) 886-5188

Daily specials are the highlight of this small country-style restaurant. Clerk-Treasurer Mosier recommends smoked pork chops, which happen to be the special on Wednesdays. Mondays feature ham and beans while broasted chicken is featured on Fridays and Sundays. Cash or check only.

Open: 11 a.m.–8 p.m. M–F, 6 a.m.–2 p.m. S, closed Su

FARMLAND

Restaurant nominated by Bernice Herndon, clerk treasurer

The Chocolate Moose

101 N. Main St., Farmland, IN 47340
(765) 468-7731

Moose Tracks, Rocky the Flying Swirl and Frozen Explosion are just some of the ice cream flavors waiting for you at The Chocolate Moose. An old-fashioned soda fountain and grill, the eatery boasts some of the tastiest tenderloin sandwiches and burgers you'll find. Order a sundae or banana split, or try a phosphate or flavored coke. Clerk-Treasurer Herndon recommends the grilled tenderloin with onion rings, or a taco salad and a chocolate shake. Cash only.

Open: 11 a.m.–9 p.m. Su–Th, 11 a.m.–10 p.m. F–S

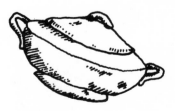

Fort Wayne

Casa D'Angelo

(south location)
3402 Fairfield Ave., Fort Wayne, IN 46807
(219) 745-7200

Known for its authentic Italian food and a locally famous house salad, Casa D'Angelo was started 17 years ago by a former FBI agent and his partner. The well-known salad comes already tossed in the special dressing, but don't ask—the recipe is a closely guarded secret. Hearty portions. Reservations (weekdays only) advised.

Open: 11 a.m.–10 p.m. M–Th, 11 a.m.–11 p.m. F–S, closed Su
MC V AmEx Di

Did you know?
The smallest city in Indiana is Woodburn—just 15 miles east of Fort Wayne—with a population 1,002. It became a city through special legislation.

Garrett

Restaurants nominated by Jennie DePaolo, clerk-treasurer

Klug's Town Tavern

127 N. Randolph, Garrett, IN 46738
(219) 357-6313

Great food served in a timely manner makes Klug's a popular spot. If you're in a hurry, they'll get you in, fed and out without delay, says Clerk-Treasurer DePaolo. The prime rib and jumbo tenderloin are delicious, and the Hoosier fries come highly recommended. Cash or check only. Sorry, no reservations.

Open: 5 a.m.–10 p.m. M–F, 5 a.m.–9:30 p.m. S, closed Su

Railroad Inn

104 N. Peters St., Garrett, IN 46738
(219) 357-5756

Railroad aficionados won't want to miss the Railroad Inn where the train memorabilia is as much a feast for the eyes as the food is for the palate. A tribute to Garrett's past, the Railroad Inn specializes in top-notch entrees such as prime rib and broasted chicken, and generous portions. Try the orange roughy or broiled cod, and don't miss the salad bar. Sorry, no reservations.

Open: 7 a.m.–10 p.m. M–Th, 7 a.m.–11 p.m. F–S, 8 a.m.–8 p.m. Su
MC V AmEx Di

GAS CITY

Restaurant nominated by Larry Leach, clerk-treasurer

Flores Mexican Food

214 W. Main St., Gas City, IN 46933
(765) 674-3222

Enjoy a bit of old Mexico at Flores, where the food is as rich as the heritage that is proudly displayed. A variety of home-cooked sauces bring out the flavors of the generous servings. From mild to hot, you'll find one you love. Try the fried beef burrito or the red burrito supreme. Clerk-Treasurer Leach recommends the Mucho Nachos. Cash only.

Open: 11 a.m.–7 p.m. M–Th, 11 a.m.–8 p.m. F–S, closed Su

GRABILL

Restaurants nominated by Joanne Sauder, councilmember

Elias Ruff House

13531 Main St., Grabill, IN 46741
(219) 627-6312

The historic Elias Ruff House is more than just a great dining experience. The restaurant is located in the original log cabin home of Mennonite minister Elias Ruff. It was built in the 1700s and moved from Pennsylvania to Indiana. The antique furniture, oil lamps and overall ambience make your dining experience an exceptional treat. All foods, such as their special Grabill chicken, are authentic to the 1800s. Councilmember Sauder recommends the Yankee pot roast.

Open: 11 a.m.–8 p.m. M–Th, 11 a.m.–9 p.m. F–S, 11 a.m.–4 p.m. Su
MC V AmEx Di

Grabill Inn

13706 Fairview Dr., Grabill, IN 46741
(219) 627-2719

If you think desert is a food group, you won't want to miss the marvelous pie and dessert bar at the Grabill Inn. It's a great restaurant for the whole family. Daily specials such as beef and noodles on Tuesday or the all-you-can-eat fish and chicken on Saturday round out a menu that is filled with dinners just like mom used to make. Councilmember Sauder recommends the prime rib and the broasted chicken.

Open: 6 a.m.–9 p.m. M–S, 8 a.m.–2 p.m. Su
MC V Di

HAMILTON

Baby Boomers

104 S. Wayne St., Hamilton, IN 46742
(219) 488-3244

Step back in time to the fabulous fifties at Baby Boomers, where you'll love the ambience and large meal portions—everything homemade! Nightly specials highlight the menu, but it's the cheeseburger basket that hits the spot for many local diners. For dessert, be sure to order a special treat from their authentic 1943 soda fountain. Sorry, no reservations, but it's worth the wait. Cash or check only.

Open: 6 a.m.–2 p.m. M–Th, 6 a.m.–8 p.m. F–S, closed Su

MARKLE

Davis Family Restaurant

165 N. Clark St., Markle, IN 46770
(219) 758-2263

Different patterns on the plates lend an element of surprise to each meal at the Davis Family Restaurant. Broasted chicken, breaded tenderloin and homemade pies are the staples here. Take a tip from the locals. Try the black raspberry pie and apple dumplings. Cash or check only.

Open: 5:30 a.m.–9 p.m. M–F, 5:30 a.m.–2 p.m. S, 7 a.m.–2 p.m. Su

MIDDLETOWN

Restaurant nominated by Dallas Hunter, councilmember

Middletown Diner

1007 W. Mill, Middletown, IN 47356
(765) 354-9284

All-you-can-eat fish and chicken specials on Friday and Saturday (respectively) make the Middletown Diner one of Councilman Hunter's favorite local hangouts. The country diner features "wholesome country cooking." Try the tenderloin sandwich. Sorry, no reservations.

Open: 5:30 a.m.–8 p.m. M–S, closed Su
MC V Di

MONTPELIER

Grandma Jo's

State Road 18 W, Montpelier, IN 47359
(765) 728-5444

You'll feel like you're at grandma's at this popular eatery. Here the local folks report they've eaten "some of the finest breaded tenderloins around" for nine years. They do all of their own breading. The lasagna and potato salad are popular selections, too, and the all-you-can-eat fish on Fridays gets rave reviews. (They have all-you-can-eat chicken on Wednesdays, too.) Banquet service available in evenings. Reservations accepted. Cash only.

Open: 6 a.m.–2 p.m. M–F, 7 a.m.–2 p.m. S–Su

New Castle

Restaurant nominated by Sherman Boles, mayor

Maxwell House

1326 Broad St., New Castle, IN 47362
(765) 521-8296

A variety of homecooked foods, casual dining and a great family atmosphere make Maxwell House tops on Mayor Boles' list. If you can't make up your mind from the menu, try the buffet, which features both hot and cold items. Reservations available.

Open: 4 a.m.–8 p.m. Th, 4 a.m.–9 p.m. F–S,
11 a.m.–3 p.m. Su, closed M–W
MC V AmEx Di

Peru

The Siding

8 West Tenth St., Peru, IN 46970
(765) 473-4041

Dine in a 1937 railroad car at The Siding, while you enjoy the beautiful Victorian railroad decor. You must try the prime rib and fresh fruit. The buffet, available at every meal, is a popular choice too. Family owned and operated for 29 years. Reservations are accepted, but credit cards are not.

Open: 11 a.m.–2 p.m. T–F, 4:30–9 p.m. T–S, closed Su–M
MC AmEx

TIPTON

Restaurant nominated by George Ogden, councilmember

Faye's Northside Café

506 N. Main St., Tipton, IN 46072
(765) 675-4191

From the minute you enter the door, you're a member of the family at Faye's. Local folks from all walks of life frequent the establishment for the delicious down-home cooking and the friendly atmosphere. Daily specials include ham and beans, meatloaf, sausage and sauerkraut, and Swiss steak. You might want to order your dessert first, though, like some of the "regulars" do—Faye's famous pies go quickly! Cash only.

Open: 5 a.m.–2 p.m. M–F, 5–10 a.m. S, closed Su

UNION CITY

Cheryl's Restaurant

415 West Chestnut, Union City, IN 47390
(765) 964-3488

Hey everybody, what time is it? It doesn't matter at Cheryl's, there's always good food. Its choice location in this Indiana/Ohio border community leaves it observing two time zones. Try the country breakfast, then stick around for lunch either on Indiana or Ohio time. If you're really hungry, eat twice! While you're eating, learn about the locals from advertisements and memorabilia adorning the walls. Reservations accepted.

Open: 4 a.m.–2 p.m. M–F, 5 a.m.–2 p.m. S, closed Su

UPLAND

Ivanhoe's

979 S. Main St., Upland, IN 46989
(765) 998-7261

With 100 shakes and 100 sundaes on the menu at Ivanhoe's, you're sure to find something to delight your tastebuds. And by the way—they have delicious sandwiches and salads, too! All food is fresh and made-to-order. Sorry no reservations and no credit cards.

Open: 10 a.m.–10 p.m. M–Th, 10 a.m.–11 p.m. F–S, 2–10 p.m. Su

WABASH

Eugenia's at the Honeywell Center

275 W. Market St., Wabash, IN 46992
(219) 563-4411

Eugenia's offers elegant dining at casual prices. Located at the Honeywell Center, site of art exhibits and a theater, Eugenia's is convenient for lunch or Sunday brunch. Serving food since 1950, this restaurant is not-for-profit, funding the Honeywell Performing Arts Center. Admire the small collection of Indiana artwork while you enjoy the soup, or perhaps one of their "bodacious" tenderloins. Or, call ahead for theater tickets and dine at the pre-concert buffet. Reservations advised.

Open: 11 a.m.–2 p.m. M–F, 11 a.m.–2 p.m.
& 5–8 p.m. (for concert events) Su
MC V AmEx Di

Did you know?
The first Indiana city to have electric street lighting was Wabash, which switched to the system in 1880.

INDEX